رمضان

خيار

رز

THE TASTE OF EGYPT

طحينا

بقدونس

ملوخية

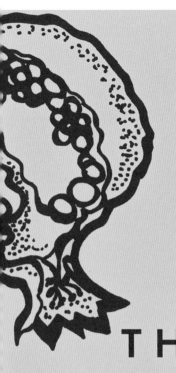

DYNA ELDAIEF

THE TASTE OF
EGYPT

HOME COOKING FROM
THE MIDDLE EAST

The American University in Cairo Press
Cairo New York

This edition first published in 2016 by
The American University in Cairo Press
113 Sharia Kasr el Aini, Cairo, Egypt
420 Fifth Avenue, New York, NY 10018
www.aucpress.com

Exclusive distribution outside Egypt and North America by I.B. Tauris & Co Ltd., 6 Salem Road,
London, W2 4BU

Dar el Kutub No. 14341/15
ISBN 978 977 416 755 3

Dar el Kutub Cataloging-in-Publication Data

    Eldaief, Dyna
        The Taste of Egypt: Home Cooking from the Middle East / Dyna Eldaief.—Cairo:
    The American University in Cairo Press, 2016
                p.   cm.
                ISBN 978 977 416 755 3
                1. Food—Egypt
                2. Cooking—Egyptian
                641.5

1 2 3 4 5   20 19 18 17 16

Cover design by **studio medlikova**

Design concept by **studio medlikova**
Design and layout by Sally Boylan

Printed in China

CONTENTS

INTRODUCTION

I am an Australian born to Egyptian parents. My father grew up in a city called Minya, south of Cairo in Egypt and emigrated to Australia in 1969. Before he made the trip he met and fell so in love with a woman that within ten days he had married her. This was my mother, and she stayed in Egypt for another year to complete her university studies in entomology before traveling to join him in the Land Down Under. My dad arrived in Australia with only one bag, containing his clothes and a single set of cutlery, but soon found himself a job and started to build up a life for himself in Australia. When my mother arrived they bought their first house together, in Melbourne. Within a few years my brother was born; three years after that I arrived on the scene, and my sister followed 18 months later.

Mum was the youngest of 18 children. (Yes, I know—that's a lot of children!) Her upbringing had given her all the skills she needed to look after us: she cut our hair, knitted us sweaters, and made dresses for us. But it wasn't until one of her sisters came to stay with us that I realized she had a talent for cooking. Her sister clearly thought so, because she lavished praise on my mother's dishes. After a while I also realized that my friends seemed fascinated with the food we ate—perhaps because it was nothing like the standard Australian fare of 'meat and three veg.' The sweets seemed to appeal to everyone (since they are mostly drenched in sugar syrup, and what's not to like about that?) but as I matured, I began to really appreciate the flavors and textures of my mother's Egyptian cooking.

In 1994 I completed high school and gained a Victorian Certificate of Education (VCE), and a year later I headed off to Monash University, Melbourne, to undertake a science degree. For the first week I tried commuting from home, but it took up to five hours a day on public transport so I relented and moved onto campus. There, I discovered a whole new world and a whole new me waiting to be unleashed. Everyone at university seemed to embrace individuality and was exploring what and how they were different. The friends I made were keen to know about me, about how I grew up, and about my culture and heritage.

Meanwhile, my mum would make meals for me and freeze them. Each weekend—whether I went home or my parents came to visit—I would stock up on home-cooked meals, which were a rare commodity for university students. I shared those meals with friends who were around at dinnertime and consequently made my way to my future husband's heart through sharing my mother's meals. I was surprised and delighted that an Aussie boy would like the food I shared, and I found that he began to drop by more and more at dinnertime. After university we married, and I realized that I couldn't reproduce my mother's range of meals because she made them without a recipe. It was then that I decided to write a cookbook, made up of the recipes that my mother cooked for us when I was growing up.

It is difficult to explain the challenges involved in putting to paper recipes that someone else has prepared for many years without any measurements. My mother would say that you work out whether a dish is right by seeing what it looks like, smells like, and tastes like. How could I argue with that? But then again, how could I portray precisely in words a smell or taste that encompassed all her years of cooking experience? This was my task, and I have endeavored to capture the tastes of these dishes while also recording the ingredients and quantities required to produce them. In practice, this often involved many attempts at preparing each dish. It has also allowed me to formulate my own tastes and preferences for the dishes I first knew as a child, and over the many years of practice I have changed and molded these to my own unique versions.

I also found out that a particular dish may be known by different names from one region in

Egypt to another. My father, who grew up in Minya, referred to certain dishes with entirely different names from those used by my mother, who was from Cairo. For the sake of consistency I have, as much as possible, used the names of dishes as my mother referred to them. To further complicate things, different regions in Egypt may prepare the same dish in different ways—by adding tomato sauce or tomato paste to *molokhiya* (page 120), for instance. There is no particular version that is more accurate than another; each one simply represents the tastes of a region, household, or cook. For instance, *molokhiya* can be prepared using beef, chicken, or even rabbit, all of which my mother tried at one time or another. I once asked my mother and several family friends how they made *basbousa* (pages 132–37) and ended up with an entirely different recipe from each person. One included almonds, another used coconut, and a third was made with yogurt instead of milk. I have made all three versions, as well as coming up with a fourth, completely dairy-free version, so that my daughter could eat *basbousa* too. I was very pleased to hear that my stepmother thought my dairy-free version was the best she had ever tasted (I had secretly thought that myself). It is imperative therefore, to keep this in mind when comparing Egyptian recipes, and to remember that when a recipe appears to be slightly different, this does not make it less authentic.

COOKING FOR KIDS

So many Egyptian dishes are great for kids. *Molokhiya* is a green soup that is served over rice or with broken bits of bread in it and I am yet to meet a child who will not eat it. All the kids I know who have tried it absolutely love it. Funnily enough, the only person I know who would not eat it was my mother. She made it often because we grew the leaves for *molokhiya*, the main ingredient of the soup, at home, and my dad loves it. The green leaves are mucilaginous when cooked, which may not appeal to some but perhaps explains why the kids love it. It's a great dish for babies too, as it is so easy to swallow.

All the variations of *tabikh* (page 68) are great for kids, as they are made in a pressure cooker or slow cooker and so produce wonderfully tender meat. *Macarona forn* (page 90) is a baked pasta dish that is another big hit with kids. The zucchini and eggplant versions (*kusa bi-l-beshamel*, page 84; and *mesa'aa*, page 82) are easy for little toddlers to eat, especially when mashed together with cooked rice or couscous. *Ul'as* (page 122) is a dish made using taro tubers, which is also great mashed together with rice, as is *kofta bi-l-dem'a* (page 70), meatballs cooked in a tomato-based sauce. For children who like finger foods, such as my little munchkin, stuffed vine leaves (*mahshi wara 'enab*, page 74) are great for little fingers to hold, as is the Egyptian omelet ('*eggah*, page 48), when cut into strips. Falafel (*ta'miya*, page 52) is a winner too.

TAKING PART IN *THE TASTE*

Just after my third child was born, I was contacted by a media company from the Middle East inviting me to take part in a TV program called *The Taste*. This is a cooking show where contestants prepare a series of dishes for four judges, who then rate the cooks based on blind tastings of just one spoonful from each dish. Originally it was to be filmed in Lebanon, but then the production shifted to Cairo. Realizing what an amazing opportunity this represented—not only to take part in the show, but also to experience Egypt and catch up with relatives I had not seen in years—I accepted the offer, and in September 2014 was en route to Cairo.

Filming the show turned out to be a wonderful experience. I met amazing people from throughout the Middle East (it turned out that I was the only contestant from elsewhere), and I gained an amazing mentor in Bethany

Khedy. The challenge was especially great for me because my spoken Arabic is fairly basic and my understanding of written Arabic is virtually non-existent—so reading names on ingredients was near on impossible! Despite these challenges I survived the experience, learned a huge amount, and managed to see some of the amazing sights of Egypt, as well as some of my relatives from both sides of the family.

All of these experiences spurred me on to complete and compile the recipes that now make up this book. I hope that they are enjoyed for their exceptional taste, rather than scrutinized for their accuracy or authenticity, as variation in Egyptian cooking is as wide as the Nile River is long. My aim is to give a glimpse into my passion for Egyptian food and family, and the need to have plenty of both at the table.

BASICS

INGREDIENTS

Egyptian food encompasses simple flavors and methods of cooking, and most of the ingredients should be relatively easy to locate in any major supermarket. Smaller grocers and delicatessens may also stock many of the items. The most common ingredients, such as lentils, rice, vermicelli noodles, and semolina are generally easy to track down, but more unusual items may be trickier to find, especially in rural areas. Many cities have districts where Asian, Indian, or Mediterranean foods are more common, and these food retailers can be a great resource. I once had great difficulty finding *kataifi*, finely spun pastry that is used in making *konafa* (pages 140–42), and I must have made over a dozen calls to shops and supermarkets trying to find it locally. In the end I drove to a suburb that had a large Greek population, and the first shop I passed had some *kataifi* in their freezer. I saw it again in several others as I walked around the area. If you plan on making a few dishes at the same time, it is probably worth tracking down a delicatessen or grocer that sells Mediterranean ingredients so you can buy them all in one place.

I have also found that many Asian grocery shops sell vegetables such as taro, okra, and artichokes, which rarely make an appearance in my local supermarket. A large market can be great too. In Melbourne, I have found that the easiest way of purchasing meat from a market is to plan ahead to find out which stall stocks what, from rabbit, pigeon (squab), oxtails, and liver to fish of all shapes and sizes.

MEAT

Meat is a must in Egyptian households. I don't know of any vegetarian Egyptians (although I am sure that they do actually exist somewhere—perhaps this is the first culinary oxymoron!). Meat was the main ingredient in many of the dishes we had at home. My mum would often use a pressure cooker as it dramatically reduces the cooking time, so if you are cooking these dishes using conventional pots,

a heavy-based one would be best. Usually meat dishes are served with white rice *(roz)* and salad at the table.

Beef and chicken are the main meats eaten in Egypt—there is little fish or lamb as these are expensive. Pork is not eaten in Egypt as it is a Muslim country. Game such as rabbit and pigeon are eaten, although less often than beef or chicken. Thinking of pigeon makes me remember the time I visited my family in Egypt when I was 12 years old. We stayed with an aunt in Minya, my dad's hometown, and one afternoon we went to a livestock market where all kinds of animals were for sale. We went to buy pigeon, so we stopped at a stall that had pigeons in a cage and started selecting a few. My sister and I spent time comparing the details of each bird and then each of us selected our favorite. We couldn't wait to take them home as our new pets. We spent several days looking after them, making sure they had food and water, and spending time with them every day after returning home from our travels. Little did we know that one afternoon we would return to find the bathroom where the pigeons had been kept sparkling clean, with no sign of our beloved pets. Being called to the table for the main meal of the day still didn't trigger any suspicions until we saw a plate full of small bodies boiled and fried about the size of say . . . pigeons! This was a very real lesson for us that animals are a source of food, and meat is not just something that appears on the supermarket shelves. In many countries rabbit and pigeon are not common sources of meat, but they can be found at some butchers, so I have included a recipe for rabbit and pigeon, or 'squab' as it is also widely known.

Along the same lines, I also recall a time when I was about seven or eight years old, and my uncle came to visit us in Australia from the USA. He bought a little gosling for each family member, which were then raised in our backyard. For various reasons only one grew to adulthood and it was mine. It turned out to be a very big, male goose that had a temper and would attack people (mainly my father) every time someone ventured into the backyard. This goose was so fierce that he would peck holes in the wellingtons my father wore to protect himself. One fateful afternoon, while all the kids were at school, my father stepped into the backyard with his wellingtons on, armed with a kitchen knife. Although the goose initially went on the attack, he soon saw the knife and backed away. Of course this is a terrible story, because it can only end in a roast bird and utterly devastated children. I still recall walking into the kitchen and telling my mother I couldn't find my pet in the backyard, only to discover that she was plucking something in the sink. The pennies dropped and frankly so did I. That was the last time we had outdoor pets.

I have written the meat recipes based on enough food for four people, but the quantities can be varied according to the number of people to be served, as well as personal taste and preference. Butter, or ghee (clarified butter), is used abundantly in these dishes, but for a healthier meal you could use vegetable oil instead.

EQUIPMENT

Egyptian cookery isn't technically demanding on the whole, so there's no need to buy special equipment, but it's good to find the cooking methods that suit you. When I was growing up, my mother made certain dishes a certain way. *Tabikh* (page 68) was always made using a pressure cooker—this was my mum's way. I, on the other hand, don't have one, and despite several attempts at buying one, still find myself relying on a heavy-based pot. This is an oversight that I really should remedy, because the dish made using a pressure cooker is definitely superior in flavor and texture. However, I have achieved very similar results by using a slow cooker (a recent and worthwhile addition to my kitchen). The beauty of both these appliances is that they are great for cooking cheaper cuts of meat, which is good news for all

of us, but especially for those on a budget. These cuts are often overlooked, but when cooked in a pressure cooker (40 minutes) or a slow cooker (6 to 8 hours), the result is extremely tender meat with wonderful flavor. If you don't have a pressure cooker or a slow cooker, a heavy-based pot is the next best thing. It allows for more even, less direct heat than the alternatives, and the trick is to keep a tight lid on it, so that the vapor can't escape during cooking—this precious steam carries with it all the aroma and therefore lots of flavor.

Fuul is the Egyptian word for broad beans (also known as fava beans). They have long been an Egyptian favorite and were traditionally prepared using a cooking method known as *medammis* (meaning 'buried') to make the dish known as *fuul medammis* (page 46). This traditionally involved burying a sealed pot of water and beans under hot coals. Since the fourth century, *fuul medammis* has also been made in a metal container fixed over the glass hood of a kerosene lamp, which is left overnight to slow-cook the beans. Making the dish my mum's way involved using a special metal pot that was tall, lidded, and purpose-specific. I never saw it used for anything else. Its main attribute was that it allowed for slow cooking over four or five hours, so you could use either a slow cooker, a normal lidded pan (allowing extra cooking time), or a pressure cooker (which will reduce the cooking time significantly). Cooking times vary depending on the type of pot used and the amount of beans being cooked, but the result should be beans that are very tender all the way through, almost to the point of falling apart. As a last resort—or if you're in a hurry—you could buy canned, pre-cooked broad beans, which still work well.

Some of the recipes in this book call for minced meat, and you can buy mincer attachments for electrical mixers. My mum used one of these to make *kobeba* (page 58), a dish that combines minced meat, wheat, and onions. I have also used a food processor in its place with satisfactory results.

Traditionally, people in Egypt take a plateful of homemade biscuits to family and friends when they visit, particularly at Christmas—it is symbolic of taking good blessings to the household for the year ahead. So making sweets, cakes, and biscuits is very common in the Egyptian household. If you would like to follow this tradition, as I do, you're likely to end up making a fairly large amount of biscuits, so it may be worth investing in a mixer (which is also useful for making cakes and bread dough) and a biscuit press. For many years I made all my biscuits by hand, but it was very time-consuming. It once took me four hours to make a batch of petits fours (though that did include making, baking, filling, and dipping them). My mother and stepmother, on the other hand, used a biscuit press with skill and could turn out a dozen trays of biscuits in a fraction of the time.

Another useful tool is a vegetable corer, which can be used to prepare vegetables such as zucchini and eggplant for stuffing. Egyptian recipes tend to use the small ('finger') Lebanese eggplants, and these are easily prepared by cutting them in half and using a corer to remove the flesh. The coring tool can be found in various kitchen stores or retailers and comes in two versions: one has a pointed end, which is good for piercing the vegetable flesh, and the other has a rounded end. I prefer the rounded-end version because there is less likelihood of piercing my own flesh!

BASIC RECIPES

There are a few recipes that warrant highlighting because they can be used to make or accompany everyday meals. Rice, for instance, is a staple accompaniment, and it was often served as part of our main meals at home. Lebanese or flat bread can be used as a substitute but I prefer rice. Yogurt is another recipe I have placed in the basics category because it is something I can enjoy often, especially with pureed fruit. Ghee was used solely in my mum's cooking and I do like to use it for the beautiful taste it has compared to oil, but you can easily substitute oil when making main dishes for a healthier version. Pickles are another frequent feature at the table. Olives, cucumber, carrot, and turnips are placed in a bowl and people can help themselves. We had pickles on the table at dinnertime or even breakfast on the weekend when we had a big Egyptian spread.

ممنوع وقوف السيارات

بامية

Zabadi | Natural Yogurt

Yogurt is a great staple—my mum would make it in a really big pickling jar and use it to make *salatit zabadi* (page 37). It is not as difficult to make as you might think, and once you know how, you may never go back to buying it. Just as in the supermarket, you can make the yogurt in many varieties by adding other ingredients, such as sugar, honey, pureed strawberries, macerated raspberries, passion-fruit pulp, and so on. If you prefer low-fat yogurt, start with low-fat milk, but if you prefer the flavor of whole milk, use that with the starter yogurt. Don't use milk close to the 'use by' date as this is not reliable for producing yogurt. The starter yogurt is easily obtained by buying a small tub of unflavored, natural, or Greek yogurt. After making each batch of your own yogurt, store some of it in a jar in the fridge to act as your starter; this will give you a continuous supply of homemade yogurt.

It may take a few attempts to get this process right. If the milk is heated too much, this may kill the bacteria so the yogurt won't set. I never saw my mother use a thermometer but I have tried to make yogurt several times without one and had mixed results, so I highly recommend buying a cooking thermometer to take out the guesswork. You will also need a one-liter (35-fl oz) container or jar with a lid and something warm to wrap around it, such as a woolen blanket.

Makes: 4 cups (1 liter)

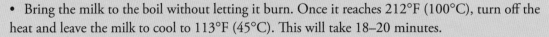

INGREDIENTS

3 tablespoons starter or plain yogurt
4 cups (1 liter) of milk

• Bring the milk to the boil without letting it burn. Once it reaches 212°F (100°C), turn off the heat and leave the milk to cool to 113°F (45°C). This will take 18–20 minutes.

• Add the starter yogurt to the container and stir it until it becomes runny. Remove the skin that forms on the milk and discard.

• Add a tablespoon of milk at a time and stir it into the yogurt. After 4 or 5 spoons, add the yogurt to the milk in the pan and stir.

• Pour all the milk back into the container, cover it with a lid, and wrap it in a blanket. Leave it in a warm place such as the bottom of a pantry for at least 10 hours or overnight. It should be wonderfully thick and creamy.

• Place the yogurt in the refrigerator—it will become sour if left out of the fridge for more than 24 hours.

VARIATION

You can make yogurt using a commercial yogurt maker. This acts like a thermos bottle, insulating the warmed milk and providing the bacteria with optimal conditions to multiply. When using a yogurt maker, make the yogurt following the method above, but instead of pouring the mixture into a container to ferment overnight, place it into your yogurt maker and follow the manufacturer's instructions.

Samna | Ghee

Ghee, or *samna*, is clarified butter. It is made by melting butter to remove the milk solids, which burn when butter is heated for too long. Ghee does not need to be kept in the fridge (in fact, my mother never did), as it does not become rancid and it is far superior to butter for use in cooking as it can be heated to high temperatures without burning. I used to loiter around the kitchen when my mum was making ghee because the smell of melted butter is just delightful and I used to love breathing in the aroma. Of course there was also the delight of eating fresh bread dipped into the salty butter residue after the ghee was poured off.

You can prepare ghee yourself by melting butter in a saucepan and removing the white milk solids that come to the surface. If using unsalted butter, there will be two layers: the milk solids and pure butter. If you begin with salted butter, there will be three separate layers: the milk solids, the pure butter, and salt. My mum would melt 2–3 kg (4½–6½ lb) at a time, but you can make as much or as little as you like.

Makes: 400 g (14 oz)

INGREDIENTS
500 g (1 lb) butter, cubed

• Melt the butter in a large, heavy-based pot or saucepan. As the milk solids rise to the surface, remove them along with any foam and discard.

• Keep skimming the surface until the butter is clear. This may take a while, but don't be tempted to rush this stage. Stirring can help the milk solids rise, so stir as often as you need. Once no more white material appears on the surface, the ghee is ready.

• Carefully pour off the clear, yellow ghee into a heatproof glass jug or container, leaving behind any salt that may have settled on the bottom of the pan. The ghee will be hot, so leave it to cool to room temperature before covering and storing.

Mikhallil | Mixed Pickles

In Egypt, pickled vegetables are served as an accompaniment to most meals, even breakfast. Often a hot breakfast of eggs, *fuul medammis* (page 46), *ta'miya* (page 52), feta cheese, bread, and *mikhallil* is normal in the Egyptian household. We usually had a breakfast like this at the weekend when everyone was home and there was no rush to get out of the house for school or work. You can buy ready-to-eat pickles from Mediterranean delicatessens and some supermarkets, but the most delicious ones are those made at home, as my mother used to do. You can source pickling jars from kitchenware retailers and homeware stores, or you can reuse glass jars such as jam jars. Ensure they have been well washed and dried; it is best to sterilize the jars before using them by boiling them for 10 minutes or putting them through a dishwasher cycle.

Pickles can be made up of single vegetables, such as cucumbers or beetroot or a mix, including carrot. I've used a particular selection of vegetables in the recipe below, but use whatever vegetables you think would be good and experiment with others.

Makes: 4 cups (1 liter)

INGREDIENTS
2 cloves garlic, peeled and crushed
2 cups (500 ml) white vinegar
2 cups (500 ml) water
150 g (½ cup) sea salt
½ small cauliflower, cut into florets
2 Lebanese cucumbers, thickly sliced, or 2 baby 'pickling' cucumbers, left whole
2–3 carrots, peeled and thickly sliced
1 tablespoon mustard seeds (optional)

• To make the pickling fluid, combine the garlic, vinegar, water, and salt in a jug and stir until the salt dissolves.

• Distribute the vegetables and mustard seeds among a few glass jars (or 1 large one, capable of holding 4 cups/1 liter) and cover them with the liquid, filling to the brim. Seal and leave for at least 1 week; they can remain unopened for many months. Once opened, the pickle jars will keep in the fridge for a few weeks, as long as the vegetables remain steeped in the pickling liquid.

VARIATION

Pickled turnip is a traditional staple in Egypt and it was my mum's favorite. You may have seen these beautiful pink pickles in an Egyptian or Turkish restaurant. To make your own, cut small turnips into quarters and place them in a jar with the pickling fluid (above) and slices of beetroot, which act like a dye.

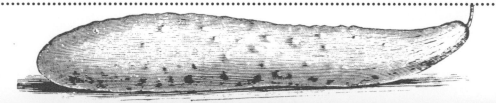

Zatun | Pickled Olives

In our house, olives were pickled in bulk. A visit to the market might be rewarded with a 10 kg (22 lb) box of green olives, which would bring joy for many months when pickled. Olives pickled using this recipe can be kept unopened for well over a year. Once opened, take out the olives you require using a slotted spoon and keep the remainder in the jar covered with the pickling juice. They will keep for several weeks once opened in the fridge.

Makes: 2 kg (4½ lb)

INGREDIENTS
2 kg (4½ lb) fresh green olives
2 celery sticks
4–6 tablespoons salt
1 lemon, sliced
Juice of 8–10 lemons

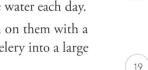

- Wash the olives and leave them covered with water for three days, changing the water each day.
- After the third day, drain the water and split the olives, either by pressing down on them with a rolling pin or cutting 2 slits into each one using a knife. Place the olives and the celery into a large pickling jar.
- Make up salty water by adding salt to 6 cups (1½ liters) of water and stirring to dissolve. Fill a third of the jar with lemon juice and then fill the remainder with the salty liquid. Once full, add a few slices of lemon on the top and seal. Leave it in a cool, dark place for several months before using.

Shorbit firakh |
Essential Chicken Stock

My mother would always make her own chicken stock and even though stock cubes, stock liquids, and stock powders are readily available in supermarkets, I love to make my own stock too. Often the recipe that calls for stock will have the chicken served alongside it as part of the meal.

Makes: 4–5 cups (1–1¼ liters)

INGREDIENTS
6 cups (1½ liters) water
1 chicken, jointed, or 4–6 chicken Maryland cuts (legs with thighs attached)
1 large onion, peeled and a cross cut into the top
Pinch or two of salt
Pinch of pepper
1 bay leaf

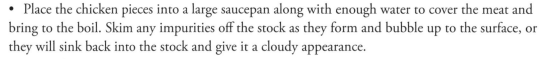

• Place the chicken pieces into a large saucepan along with enough water to cover the meat and bring to the boil. Skim any impurities off the stock as they form and bubble up to the surface, or they will sink back into the stock and give it a cloudy appearance.

• Add the onion, salt, pepper, and bay leaf. Reduce the heat and simmer gently for 45 minutes or until the meat is tender. If making a large batch, simmer for 1–1½ hours to reduce the water content and develop the flavor.

• Strain and reserve the liquid, then leave the stock to cool. The fat will rise to the surface and solidify, so if you would like to remove it, it is easy to skim it off the top. However, there is a lot of flavor in the fat, so I don't usually remove any unless there is a very thick layer of it.

• The stock can be stored in the fridge for up to 4 days, or frozen for up to 2 months. When using it, always bring it to the boil first before using it. The stock can be used in many ways, including rice *(roz)* dishes, *molokhiya* (page 120), and *fatta* (page 118).

COOK'S TIP
If you miss some of the impurities and your stock ends up being slightly cloudy, just strain the liquid though several layers of muslin cloth into a clean bowl. The resulting stock will be beautifully clear and delicious.

Double Chicken Stock

This 'double stock' method produces an absolutely delicious, full-flavored chicken stock that is bound to make any dish taste better. It takes approximately the same time as the Essential Chicken Stock, but uses twice as many ingredients.

Makes: 3–4 cups (¾–1 liter)

INGREDIENTS
Essential Chicken Stock (page 20)
½ chicken or 2–3 chicken Maryland cuts (legs with thighs attached)
1 large onion, peeled and a cross cut into the top
1 bay leaf
Pinch of salt
Pinch of freshly ground pepper

• Place the stock into a large saucepan along with the chicken and enough water to cover the meat and bring to the boil. Skim any impurities off the stock as they form and bubble up to the surface. Add the whole onion and bay leaf. Reduce the heat and simmer gently for 45 minutes or until the meat is tender.

• Remove the cooked chicken and taste for seasoning. Add salt and pepper if required.

• Strain and reserve the liquid, then leave the stock to cool before refrigerating or freezing.

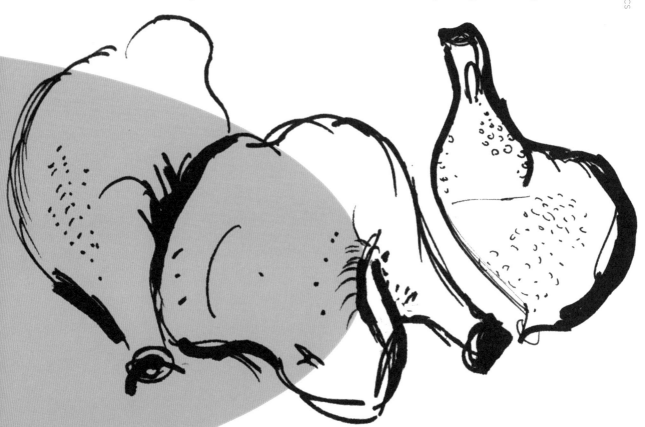

Roz bi-l-shiʻriya | Rice with Vermicelli

Rice is a staple in Egypt and it was the first thing that my mother taught me to cook. I learned how important it was to follow her instructions exactly in order to produce rice that was well cooked, that's to say, firm, not hard, and well separated, but never soggy. An Asian friend commented on it the first time I made it for her. She was intrigued by this rice because the rice grains are well-cooked but remain individual, which is quite different from the steamed or sticky rice she is accustomed to. This rice was also an absolute favorite of the next-door neighbor's children, so much so that my mother would prepare a large quantity of it to take with us when we visited them as adults.

The rice in Egypt is short and plump, but this recipe works well with long-grain rice too—especially jasmine or basmati rice. If you are health-conscious, choose basmati rice as it has a lower glycemic index (GI). This means that it releases glucose into the bloodstream at a slow, sustainable rate rather than a rush and so is much better for you. If you are trying to lower your cholesterol level, substitute vegetable oil in place of the ghee (samna).

You can also play with the flavor of rice by substituting infused oil for the ghee and adding some stock. The best flavor comes from using the stock left over from roasting a chicken or lamb. Simply pour off the roasting juice and keep it in the fridge, where it will form a layer of fat and a layer of jelly. Then remove the fat layer and use the stock in this recipe.

One last piece of advice: I recall that during my first effort at cooking rice I made the mistake of stirring the rice during cooking—this is an absolute no no. Mum refused to eat it (knowing exactly what I'd done) so it was the first and only time I made that error!

Serves: 4 –6

INGREDIENTS
1 tablespoon ghee
1 small handful crushed, dried vermicelli noodles
400 g (14 oz) jasmine or basmati rice
2 cups (500 ml) water
1 cup (250 ml) chicken stock
Pinch of sea salt flakes

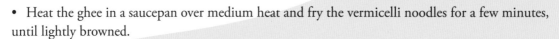

• Heat the ghee in a saucepan over medium heat and fry the vermicelli noodles for a few minutes, until lightly browned.

• Add the rice and stir continuously for 3–4 minutes until the rice grains are coated in butter and translucent. Some rice will turn opaque or white, which is fine, but do not allow any grains to burn. Add water, stock, and salt to taste.

• Bring to the boil over a high heat, stirring occasionally. Reduce the heat, cover, and simmer for 20 minutes. Do not stir the rice once it is simmering. The rice will develop characteristic little tunnels while cooking. Remove from heat, stir thoroughly, and serve.

COOK'S TIPS

If you prefer, you can use chicken or vegetable stock cubes or powder dissolved in water, but be sure to taste the liquid before adding any salt. There is no need to wash the rice using this method of cooking, as the rice bought in supermarkets is perfectly clean and the starch doesn't need to be washed away. As a general rule, use 1½ cups (375 ml) of liquid for each cup of rice for the best result.

Roz ahmar | Salmon-colored Rice

I really like this rice, perhaps for the lovely pink color it acquires, or for the subtle infusion of the tomato and onion flavor. Whatever the reason, it is a fantastic accompaniment for fish, whether freshly fried, baked, grilled, or even canned (as I have tried once or twice).

As I mention in Rice with Vermicelli (*roz bi-l-shi'riya*, page 22) the rice grains can vary considerably in their size, starch content, and nutritional value. I prefer to use basmati rice as it cooks well and is slightly better nutritionally than other white grains of rice.

While ghee or butter is used commonly in Egyptian cooking, this rice is made without it. I prefer to use olive oil here because it does not overpower the tomato and onion flavor.

Serves: 4

INGREDIENTS
1 tablespoon olive oil
1 small onion, finely chopped
300 g (10½ oz) white long-grain rice
3 tablespoons thickened tomato paste
2¼ cups (560 ml) water
Pinch of salt
Chopped parsley, to serve

• Heat the oil in a saucepan over medium heat, add the onion, and fry until golden brown. Add the rice and stir for 2 minutes, then add the tomato paste and cook for a further minute.

• Pour in the water and taste for seasoning, adding salt as required. Stir and bring to the boil. Reduce the heat, stir, then cover and simmer for 20–25 minutes, stirring once toward the end of cooking.

• Remove from heat and serve with cooked fish, garnished with parsley.

'Eish mihammas | Pita Chips

I remember going to a real Egyptian wedding in Australia when I was in my early teens. It was the only one that stands out in my memory, for several reasons, but one of them was that it was the first time that I came across pita chips made this way. I remember it distinctly because I couldn't stop eating them and they were only the first course! They are particularly appealing presented on a platter with natural yogurt (*zabadi*, page 16), *baba ghanoug* (page 39), or *hummus bi-t-tahina* (page 38).

I walked home from school when I was a teenager and always had the munchies when I got home. My staple snack was buttered pita or flatbread, grilled until crunchy. Sometimes I added slices of cheese and onion before grilling and then enjoyed savoring the melted, stretchy cheese that developed on top. As an adult I have experimented and found that the best pita chips are the fried ones—they are golden and super-crunchy. For a sensational twist on tradition serve these with *fuul medammis* (page 46). You can also use any kind of flatbread in place of pita bread for this recipe.

Serves: 6–8

INGREDIENTS
5 pieces (1 packet) white pita bread
Vegetable oil, for frying
Sea salt flakes

• Cut each pita bread into quarters, and then cut each quarter into half.

• Heat some oil in a small- to medium-sized pan. The oil is hot enough for frying when it can brown a small piece of bread in 10–15 seconds. Gently place 2 or 3 pieces of bread at a time into the oil and fry until just golden in color, then turn over and cook the other side.

• When both sides are lightly colored, remove and place on paper towel. Lightly sprinkle with salt flakes and serve.

SNACKS
AND
STARTERS

حمص

اصن

SNACKS AND STARTERS

While this section includes nibbles or snacks, it also contains starters, but then I don't tend to restrict recipes to a particular course at home. I have made *'eggah* for breakfast as well as for a light dinner, and while it is customary to have *kobeba* as a starter or entrée in Egypt, at home I make it as a main meal and serve it along with a salad.

Growing up, we often had pumpkin or watermelon seeds to nibble on during the day, and roasted peanuts or pomegranate would be our usual preference for the evening snack. I still love to sit and unleash the kernels from a pomegranate, but now I like to share the task with my kids, as they enjoy it too. Pity I don't have a pomegranate tree, as they provide such an abundance of fruit that my children would have plenty to occupy their time.

The snacks in this section are readily available in supermarkets in Australia so they should not be difficult to find, but a nut shack or grocer that stocks dried beans will surely stock these seeds too. They may not be your first choice of snack over crisps or chocolate but are definitely worth a try for a more natural and nutritional snack option.

The recipes in this section are the little dishes that surprise and add variety to the table. They are also simple yet full of flavor. You might eat them at any time of day, and you might eat them on their own or with other dishes. I hope that you find them as enjoyable as I have over the years.

Fuul sudani | Salt-roasted Peanuts

At home we often had something to nibble on after the evening meal while relaxing or watching television. This was usually watermelon or pumpkin seeds (page 31) that could be cracked open and eaten, or a bowl of mixed nuts. In summer, fruit and grapes were often the snack of choice, and in winter, chestnuts and roasted peanuts *(fuul sudani)* were favorites too. Roasting peanuts is quite easy to do and they are lovely to have warm on a cold winter's night. It was always dad who would be the kitchen boss when peanuts were roasted, then we would sit together peeling them and eating them to our heart's content. The shells and peanut skins always meant a vacuum cleaner was required afterward, because for some reason they always ended up everywhere! This recipe uses shelled peanuts, which definitely cuts down on the cleaning up.

Makes: 500 g

INGREDIENTS
1 tablespoon sea salt
½ cup (125 ml) water
500 g (1 lb) raw, shelled peanuts

- Preheat the oven to a moderate temperature: 180°C (350°F/Gas mark 4). Add the salt to the water and mix to dissolve.
- Place the peanuts on an oven tray, pour the salted water over them, and mix to coat.
- Place the tray of peanuts in the oven and stir them occasionally during cooking. They are ready when lightly brown and roasted through (around 15–20 minutes).
- Remove the peanuts from the oven, place in a serving bowl, and leave to cool. Rub off the skin between your fingers before eating.

Lib |
Watermelon and Pumpkin Seeds

Dried pumpkin or black watermelon seeds are commonly eaten as a snack in Egypt. In summer, when watermelons are plentiful and succulent, we would always have some in the fridge, and dad would cut one up after dinner. So getting watermelon seeds was very easy then! We would collect them, wash them, and leave them on newspaper to dry in the sun for a few days. This recipe provides a way of roasting seeds wherever you live, and whatever the weather. It can be used for roasting watermelon or pumpkin seeds. To eat, place the small end of the seed between your front teeth and break the seal. Continue to bite along the join until halfway down the seed, then remove the seed from the skin and eat the inside part.

Makes: 250g (½ lb)

INGREDIENTS
½ tablespoon sea salt
½ cup (125 ml) water
250g (½ lb) watermelon or pumpkin seeds, washed and dried

- Preheat the oven to 180°C (350°F/Gas mark 4). Add the salt to the water and mix to dissolve.
- Place the seeds on an oven tray, pour the salted water over them, and mix to coat.
- Place the tray of seeds in the oven and stir them occasionally during cooking. Check them often and remove when lightly brown and roasted through (5–10 minutes).

Tirmis | Lupini Beans

Lupini beans are part of the legume family, which means that when they 'go to seed' they make pods filled with beans. The seeds, or beans, contain bitter alkaloids that can be poisonous if the beans are not treated properly. In order to make lupini beans edible, they must be soaked in a brine solution to draw out the alkaloids. This takes time and patience, but the reward is a snack with a great flavor that is also very high in protein—making them a good choice for vegans and vegetarians. Lupini beans can also be found for sale with brine in jars (like olives and pickles), which is a good option if you don't have time to prepare them yourself.

Makes: 200 g (7 oz)

INGREDIENTS
200 g (½ lb) dried lupini beans
5 tablespoons sea salt

- In a large bowl, dissolve 1 tablespoon of the salt in 4 cups (1 liter) of water. Add the lupini beans, making sure they are covered with the salt water, and leave them to soak overnight.

- The next morning, drain the water from the beans, and repeat the process—adding 4 cups (1 liter) of fresh water and 1 tablespoon of salt to the beans. Leave to soak overnight.

- Repeat this process a further 3 times, each time using fresh water and salt, so that the beans are soaked in fresh, salty water for 5 days in a row.

- After the fifth overnight soaking, drain the beans and place them in a serving bowl. To eat, make a small tear in the skin with your teeth (or gently rub the bean between forefinger and thumb) to remove the skin, then pop the seed directly into your mouth. The lupini should not taste bitter, as the alkaloids should have been leached out. If any trace of bitterness remains, repeat the soaking process for another 24 hours, then re-test for bitterness. Lupini will keep in the fridge for several weeks if kept in a brine solution.

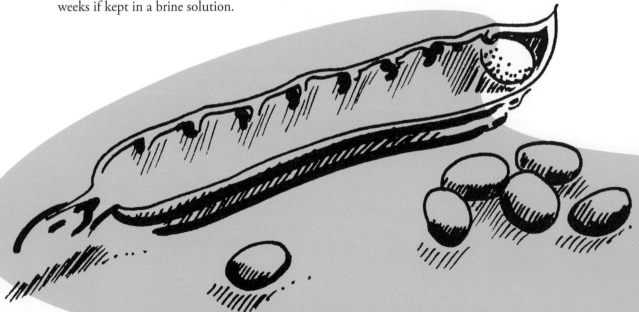

Rumman | Pomegranate

I love this fruit. The kernels are like tiny, edible, sparkling gems. When I was a child, we had a tree in the backyard that produced an abundance of pomegranate. I grew up having the 'job' of peeling the skin and removing the plump bright red seeds from within, which was a task that I always found relaxing and enjoyable. Now I have to battle my kids as they fight me for the job! Mostly it's a joint effort as we sit down together with two bowls in front of us and remove the seeds.

There are several ways to remove the seeds from a pomegranate. One way is to cut the top and scoop out the seeds with a spoon. I like to cut a circle out of the top and slowly peel away the skin, removing the segments and then the kernels carefully so they are not bruised. If you feel less confident with a knife, the following method works well. Also, by working underwater, there is less chance of the highly staining juice damaging your clothes.

I can't recall any recipes my mother would use these in but I like to use them as a garnish for a vegetable salad or a dried-fruit compote such as *khoshaf* (page 154).

Makes: 1 cup (6 oz)

INGREDIENTS
1 pomegranate

- Cut the top (the crown) off the pomegranate, then score the flesh into four sections, cutting vertically along the pomegranate skin.
- Gently pull apart the sections, breaking the pomegranate first in half and then into quarters.
- Place the sections into a bowl of water and use your fingers to roll the seeds away from the skin. As you work, the lighter pith and membranes will rise to the top of the water. Pick these out, then drain the contents of the bowl, retaining the pomegranate seeds. Tip the seeds onto a paper towel to dry slightly before using in a recipe, or simply eat the beautiful gem-like fruit immediately.

> COOK'S TIP
>
> It may be difficult to find a ripe fruit. I pick the fruit from a tree when the fruit has split open, but in the supermarket you rarely find them already open. Look for a fruit that has a firm skin (as it ages, the skin gets thinner and starts to wrinkle) and a deep red color.

Teen shoki | Prickly Pear

In some parts of Australia the landscape is dotted with cacti. There was so much of a problem with prickly pear cacti at one stage that the moth *Cactoblastis cactorum* was introduced from South America to control it, as the larvae of the moth eats the prickly pear.

Strangely, even though prickly pear is readily available on wild cacti in Australia, most Aussies are totally unaware of how delicious its golden or ruby-red fruit is. The same is true in many of the countries in which the cactus grows wild, from the USA, Mexico, and South America to Africa and parts of the Mediterranean. The fruit itself is sweet, and like pomegranate it has an abundance of seeds throughout. Admittedly, a little caution is required in its preparation because of all the prickles. I peel these fruits in one sitting to reduce the risk of getting prickles, which is a hazard of the job even with rubber gloves on. I use a pair of tongs and sharp knife with kitchen gloves on. I suggest keeping kids out of the kitchen until they are fully peeled. Collecting the pears in the wild, though, is great fun—I have taken my sons on little expeditions to hunt down wild-growing prickly pear.

Serves: 2–4

INGREDIENTS
4 prickly pears

• Place a clean bowl near the kitchen sink—you will need to peel the pear over the sink then drop the peeled pear into a bowl. Wear kitchen gloves. Using tongs, hold a prickly pear in one hand, and use a knife to cut off each end of the pear. Score the skin of the pear into quarters, cutting from one end to the other.

• Use the tongs to peel away the skin from the flesh. Place the peeled pear into a clean bowl and repeat for the remaining pears.

COOK'S TIP

When buying prickly pears, select fruit that has a deep color (either red or yellow).

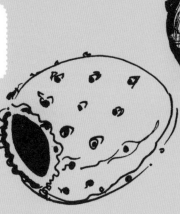

Tahina | Tahini Dip

Tahini is a sesame-seed paste that has become much more easily available in Australia than it used to be when I was growing up, and it is now sold in many supermarkets and grocery shops around the world. Many people today use it as a tasty, healthy, and dairy-free alternative to butter or margarine on an everyday basis, because tahini is high in calcium and several vitamins including vitamins E, F, and several of the B-group of vitamins. It is also a richer source of protein than milk, soya beans, sunflower seeds, and most nuts.

This recipe uses tahini paste to make a delicious dip that can be served with crisp Lebanese flatbread on a party platter with crisp crudités, or as a wonderful accompaniment to fish. The paste can be stored in the pantry in a tightly closed container for several months.

Makes: 150 g (5 oz)

INGREDIENTS
3 tablespoons tahini paste
¾ teaspoon crushed garlic
¼ teaspoon salt, or to taste
½ teaspoon ground cumin
Juice of 1 lemon or 1 tablespoon white vinegar
½ cup (125 ml) water
Small handful of fresh parsley, chopped
3–5 marinated green olives, finely chopped (optional)

• Place the tahini paste, crushed garlic, salt, cumin, and lemon juice or vinegar in a blender and mix well to form a smooth paste.

• Add water a little at a time and keep mixing well. If the mixture begins to separate or seize, add more water and keep mixing until smooth. If the mixture looks thicker than desired, add a little more water.

• Add the parsley and chopped olives, then pulse just enough to combine. Serve immediately or refrigerate.

COOK'S TIP

To make your own tahini paste, heat an oven to 180°C (350°F/Gas mark 4) and toast 700 g (25 oz) of sesame seeds for 5–10 minutes. Toss frequently and do not allow them to brown, as this will result in a bitter paste. Leave to cool, then place in a food processor with 1½ cups (375 ml) olive or vegetable oil and blend for 2 minutes. Add more oil and blend to reach a thick but pourable texture. This should yield about 560 g (20 oz).

Salatit zabadi | Yogurt Dip

Traditionally, this dip is served alongside stuffed vine leaves (*mahshi wara 'enab*, page 74) as a dipping sauce. It adds acidity to the *mahshi* as well as a lovely creaminess. In Europe and Australia it is known as tzatziki and it is available from many supermarkets, but it is such an easy dip to make that you should never need to buy it again—and it tastes delicious when freshly made. The easiest way to make *salatat zabadi* is by using shop-bought, Greek-style yogurt, which is lovely and thick, but if you make your own yogurt it can be thickened and used as well (see *Cook's Tip*, below).

Makes: 350 g (12 oz)

INGREDIENTS
1 large Lebanese cucumber, peeled
1 cup (260 g) natural Greek-style yogurt
2 cloves garlic, crushed
1–2 teaspoons dried mint, or 1 tablespoon finely chopped fresh mint

• Cut the cucumber in half lengthways and remove the seeds from the center. Removing the seeds is not essential, but they carry a lot of water, so keeping the seeds in the dip may make it thin and runny. Pat the cucumber dry using some paper towel, then finely chop or grate the flesh.

• In a bowl, combine the yogurt, cucumber, garlic, and mint, then gently mix together. Serve immediately or store in the fridge for up to a week.

COOK'S TIP

To thicken natural plain yogurt you will need to strain it using a cheese or muslin cloth. Simply place the amount of yogurt required in the center of the cloth and bring the corners of the cloth together. Tie these together using a rubber band and leave the yogurt parcel draining in a sieve over a bowl for 30 minutes to an hour (depending on the quantity) to remove some of the liquid whey. If you find that you have thickened the yogurt too much, add a little whey back in and stir it in. Do not leave the yogurt draining for the day or overnight, as you might end up with cheese!

Hummus bi-t-tahina | Hummus Dip with Smoked Paprika

Makes: 450 g (1 lb)

INGREDIENTS
150 g (5 oz) dried chickpeas
Juice of 1 lemon
2 cloves garlic, crushed
2 tablespoons olive oil
½ teaspoon ground cumin
70 g (2½ oz) tahini paste
Ground smoked paprika,
 to garnish

Tahini may be made from hulled or unhulled sesame seeds, and the two versions are different nutritionally, as well as in taste and color. Tahini made with unhulled seeds is richer in vitamins (E, F, and B) and minerals (especially calcium), and it is darker, with a stronger flavor. If you decide to use the unhulled version, start with 1 tablespoon of the paste and add more as required, as it is quite difficult to abate the flavor intensity if there is too much too begin with.

The smoked paprika in this dip is not traditional, but it adds a vibrant color, has a lovely smoky taste, and helps add flavor to the chickpeas, which are relatively flavorless. Use the paprika sparingly, though, as a little goes a long way. If you want to prepare the dip in a hurry, you could use a 400 g (14 oz) can of cooked chickpeas instead of the dried ones.

- Put the dried chickpeas in a bowl, cover with cold water, and leave overnight.
- Drain the chickpeas, place them in a saucepan, and cover with fresh water. Bring to the boil and cook on high heat for 10 minutes, then reduce the heat and simmer for 2 hours or until soft. Drain.
- Place the chickpeas in a food processor and blend to a smooth consistency. Add the lemon juice, garlic, olive oil, cumin, and tahini and blend until smooth. Taste and season as required.
- Transfer to a bowl, garnish with paprika, and serve or refrigerate. This dip will keep in the fridge for several days and is great as a butter substitute for sandwiches.

Baba ghanoug | Eggplant Dip

Makes: 340 g (12 oz)

INGREDIENTS

2 cloves garlic, unpeeled
1 large or 2 small eggplants
7 tablespoons olive oil
½ teaspoon salt, or to taste
4 tablespoons tahini
2 tablespoons chopped parsley,
 plus extra for garnishing
½ teaspoon ground cumin
Juice of 1 lemon

This is a great way to use eggplant because this spongy vegetable absorbs the flavors of garlic and cumin beautifully, while also adding texture to the dip. Traditionally, the eggplant is cooked over an open flame or roasted, but I am frying it here because I love the rich taste it develops.

Eggplant is a wonderful vegetable with a beautiful deep purple–black color and smooth skin. I grow eggplants in the garden so that I can have a fresh supply. I have found that freshly picked eggplants, even when mature, have no bitterness at all—unlike the store-bought ones, which have generally become bitter during storage. However, if you are using supermarket eggplants, you can dispel the bitterness by eliminating the liquid from the eggplant flesh. Simply cut the vegetable into long slices and sprinkle salt on the flesh. Leave it to draw out the liquid for around 30 minutes, then rinse and pat dry with a paper towel.

- Heat the oven to 180 °C (350 °F/Gas mark 4). Put the garlic on a roasting tray and roast for 15 minutes or until soft. Allow to cool, then remove the flesh from the skin.

- While the garlic is roasting, slice the eggplant into 1 cm (½ in) slices. Heat 2 tablespoons of oil in a frying pan, and add a batch of eggplant once the oil is hot. If the oil is too cool, the eggplant will soak it up rather than fry. Turn the slices often to prevent burning, cooking each batch of slices for 1–2 minutes. Aim to cook two batches, using 2 tablespoons of oil each time. Don't be tempted to crowd the pan, or the eggplant will begin to steam, rather than fry. Set each cooked batch aside to cool.

- Place the fried eggplant, roast garlic, salt, tahini, parsley, cumin, 3 tablespoons oil, and lemon juice in an electric blender or food processor and blend. Don't overblend—you're aiming for a little texture. Add a little water if the mix is too thick.

- Taste and adjust seasoning if required. Transfer to a bowl and garnish with chopped parsley. Serve with crisp Lebanese flatbread or fresh Turkish bread, or alongside barbecued meat or *kofta*.

VARIATION

If you don't want to fry the eggplant, you can cook it over an open flame—this is easy if you have a gas stove—but it may be easier to place it in the oven or under a grill. Whichever method you choose, cook the eggplant whole, with the skin on—when this becomes wrinkly and blackened, it is ready. Place it in a closed plastic bag for a few minutes to sweat, then take it out and remove the skin, which will now peel off very easily.

Salatit fasulya | Five-bean Salad

This is a wonderfully simple salad to put together. It's especially easy and quick if you use canned beans, which are also guaranteed to be soft but not mushy. Alternatively, you could use dried beans that have been soaked overnight then cooked. These must be carefully prepared, as some dried beans can be poisonous if not treated correctly. Red kidney beans, for instance, contain natural toxins called lectins that can cause stomach aches and vomiting. These are destroyed by soaking the dried beans for at least 12 hours and then boiling them vigorously for 10 or more minutes in fresh water before simmering until cooked. Tinned or canned kidney beans have already gone through this process, so they require only a rinse under fresh water before being used.

Dried beans may take up to 3 hours to cook using the conventional method, but they cook in about a third to a quarter of the time if cooked in a pressure cooker.

When judging the amount of beans you need, remember that dried beans will double in weight and volume after being soaked and cooked. So 2 cups (1 lb) dried beans will yield around 4 cups of cooked beans. Aim for a good mix of bean types—the recipe suggests five different kinds of bean, but select a mixture (or just use one type) according to your own taste. Mixed beans add a variety of flavor and color to the dish, and these beans work especially well: black-eye beans, great northern beans, red kidney beans, cannellini beans, and butter beans.

Serves: 4

INGREDIENTS
1½ tablespoons garlic-infused olive oil
½ lemon, juiced
Pinch of salt
1 cup dried beans, soaked and cooked, or 1 can of mixed beans
2–3 tablespoons chopped parsley
½ small onion, very finely chopped
2 Roma tomatoes, finely diced

- Combine the olive oil, lemon juice, and salt.
- Place the beans in a bowl and add the parsley, onion, and tomatoes.
- Mix together, pour over the dressing, and toss well just before serving.

Salatit khudar mishakkil | Green Summer Salad

A salad is a great way to include fresh vegetables as part of a healthy diet. When I was growing up, we had a salad with dinner almost every night, made up of a few core vegetables and then whatever else was available. Crisp veggies such as capsicum, green chili, and carrot add great texture and color. While I didn't grow up having avocado, its creamy texture and taste make it a great addition too. Freshly picked rocket, parsley, fennel leaves, or dill really change the flavor, and the dark green looks lovely in the salad. You can use whichever raw vegetables you like or have available and it will always make a great accompaniment to a main meal. If you want to recreate our dinner table of old, add some feta cheese, olives, and mixed pickles to the feast.

Serves: 4

INGREDIENTS
½ iceberg lettuce, finely sliced
Large handful rocket leaves
6 cherry tomatoes, halved, or 1 large tomato, chopped
½ avocado, stoned and cubed
1 Lebanese cucumber, finely sliced
½ small onion or 2 spring onions, finely sliced
1 stick celery, finely sliced
Small bunch flat-leaf parsley

Dressing
2 tablespoons extra-virgin olive oil
Juice of ½ lemon
½ teaspoon salt

- Combine the salad ingredients in a large bowl.
- Mix the oil, lemon juice, and salt in a jug to make the dressing.
- Dress the salad just before serving.

Salatit tamatim, Salatit basal | Simply Tomato, Simply Onion

Serves: 4

INGREDIENTS

1 large brown onion cut into
    quarters or eighths
Juice of ½ lemon, plus a slice
    of lemon
2 vine-ripened tomatoes
Pinch of ground cumin
Pinch of sea salt flakes
1 clove garlic, crushed (optional)

These two basic salads are an easy way to add flavor and color to a meal, and they are both lovely alongside *fuul medammis* (page 46). They were often served together at home. The acidity of the lemon reduces the potency of the onion, so a little bite of onion with *fuul medammis* in pita bread is a great combination. The tomato and cumin are great with *fuul* too, as well as with falafel (page 52). I like to use vine-ripened tomatoes in this recipe as they have a beautiful flavor. If you have access to heirloom tomatoes, this is a delicious way to use them.

• Quarter the onions and mix with the lemon juice for 10–15 minutes. Place the onion and lemon on a plate and serve.

• Quarter or thickly slice the tomatoes and sprinkle them with cumin, salt, and a little crushed garlic. Place the tomatoes on a plate and serve.

Tabboola | Parsley and Tomato Salad

Serves: 6 as a side dish

INGREDIENTS

250 g (½ lb) brown bulgur wheat

2 cups (500 ml) hot water

2 small onions or 4 spring onions, finely chopped

A few garlic chives, finely chopped

A few chopped green olives (optional)

2 large tomatoes, finely diced

½ cup flat-leaf or Italian parsley, finely chopped

¼ cup (60 ml) extra virgin olive oil

Juice of 1–2 lemons

Salt and pepper, to taste

This traditional Lebanese salad has become well known in recent years, having moved beyond the realm of Mediterranean restaurants and into supermarket deli counters, kebab shops, and takeaways. We usually had a garden salad with the evening meal at home, but at a barbecue, party, or family gathering we always had Tabboola too.

I have seen so many variations in the ratio of parsley to bulgur with this salad that I've realized this is very much down to the cook's own taste. I myself sit more on the side that treats bulgur wheat as the star, rather than the parsley, but don't get me wrong—I still add plenty of parsley. A fresh herb in a salad is always great, and parsley is fantastic because not only does it add a lovely fresh flavor but it is a wonderfully high source of vitamin A.

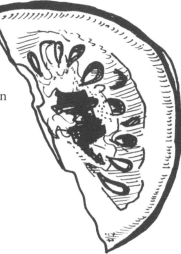

- Place the bulgur wheat in a large bowl and cover it with the hot water. Leave to stand for 1–2 hours until soft (the timing depends on the grind of the bulgur, so check the packet for instructions). Drain and squeeze out as much liquid as possible with your hands, then spread out on a clean tea towel for a few minutes to dry further.

- In a bowl, combine the bulgur, onions, chives, olives, tomatoes, parsley, olive oil, and lemon. Season to taste, adding more seasoning, lemon or oil as required. This salad should be distinctly lemony.

Salatit kharshuf | Artichoke Salad

Artichokes might seem a bit daunting to prepare, but they are not as difficult as they appear. They are time-consuming though, and at the end it seems like most of the vegetable has been wasted. But if you find yourself keen to give the fresh stuff a go, this recipe is certainly worth the effort.

Serves: 4

INGREDIENTS
4 globe artichokes
2 lemons
Sea salt flakes and freshly ground pepper
Drizzle of virgin olive oil

• Cut off the stems from the artichokes and remove any tough outer leaves (some people prefer to leave the stems on for some recipes, removing only the leaves and fibrous outer green layer).

• Cut off the top quarter of the artichoke, trimming the top leaves, and then trim the tips of the remaining leaves with scissors or a knife. This leaves the artichoke center or heart. Brush the cut surfaces with lemon juice, or soak in a bowl of lemon juice and water, to prevent browning.

• You will need to discard the fuzzy center or 'choke,' which can be done either before or after cooking. To cook, place the artichokes in boiling salted water for 20 minutes or until soft.

• Remove from the heat and leave to cool slightly. Season with salt and pepper and squeeze lemon juice on top. Drizzle with a little olive oil and serve.

Akla mishakkila | Rainbow Salad Platter

This pretty dish is basically a variety of multi-colored ingredients chopped up and placed on a platter. It is a healthy meal, because there are plenty of fresh vegetables, and it also provides a variety of protein. You can use any meats or cheeses that take your fancy. The idea is that people sit around the platter and each person assembles whatever they like on bread or crackers, and then eats it. The combinations are endless. I remember eating like this on Sunday nights growing up, and it is a family tradition that I have adopted, making this one of my favorite easy dinners for Sunday night.

I have also served this at a casual dinner party for friends. It was a big hit, because it is easy and fun. Hands start moving in all directions, picking up foods of different colors and building little towers of food which are then thrown into mouths whole or crunched and crumbled. This is definitely not a knife and fork meal, but who says they all have to be?

Serves: 4–8

INGREDIENTS

A selection of bread or crackers
A selection of cheeses, such as feta, Gouda, Parmesan, or cheddar
A selection of cooked or cured meats, such as ham, turkey, chicken, and salami
4–6 tomatoes, halved and sliced
2–3 Lebanese cucumbers, sliced
1 small onion or several radishes, very thinly sliced
4 hard-boiled eggs, sliced
Small handful marinated green or black olives, pitted
2 pickled cucumbers, sliced (optional)
2 avocados, peeled and sliced
Dips such as *hummus bi-tahina* (page 38) and *baba ghanoug* (page 39)
Steamed vegetables, such as sliced carrot or broccoli florets
Handful rocket or baby spinach leaves
2–3 small capsicum, or bell peppers (red, yellow, or green)

• Assemble all your ingredients on a few large platters, making sure that the arrangements make a wonderful rainbow effect. Place the platters on a table and ask everyone to tuck in. Eat and Enjoy!

Fuul medammis | Slow-cooked Fava Beans

This is *the* national dish in Egypt. It is delightfully tasty and suitable for everyone, including vegetarians and vegans. *Fuul* is the Egyptian word for 'broad beans' (also known as fava beans), and *medammis* is a word meaning 'buried,' which refers to the original cooking method of burying a pot of beans and water under hot coals. Today, most people prepare the dish using a slow cooker; in Egypt they often use a special *dammasa* slow cooker, which has a container of hot water on top for topping up the beans as they cook.

This dish takes me back to Saturday morning breakfasts, when my dad would get up early and get fresh bread then make a huge spread of *fuul medammis*, falafel (known as *ta'miya* in most parts of Egypt), boiled eggs, feta, pickles, olives, chopped tomatoes, and other salad items. What better way to wake up? Needless to say, my husband's first introduction to Saturday morning breakfast at my parents' house was quite a shock. He was unaccustomed to the quantity and variety of food because he grew up eating cereal with milk for breakfast (and mostly still does).

My parents always used a *dammasa* slow cooker for cooking *fuul* (as the dish tends to be known), but I don't have one. Instead, I use a heavy-based pot with a tight-fitting lid. The main rule is to use a small pot for a small amount of beans; don't use a large pot for a few beans or the liquid will quickly evaporate. If the pan you use does not have an especially tight-fitting lid, allow a little extra cooking time than given in the recipe. A pressure cooker could be used but it is not recommended, as the beans tend to be overcooked, becoming mushy and almost soup-like. A slow cooker would be better and quicker, but the quickest and easiest (cheating) option would be to buy canned broad beans.

Fuul can be made in advance, cooled, then refrigerated for up to 2 days or frozen for several months. Thaw out in the fridge overnight. Then heat and add the remaining ingredients.

Serves: 2

INGREDIENTS
160 g (5 oz) dried broad beans
2 tablespoons extra virgin olive oil
1 clove garlic, crushed
1 teaspoon cumin powder
Juice of 1 lemon
Sea salt flakes
Pinch of freshly ground black pepper

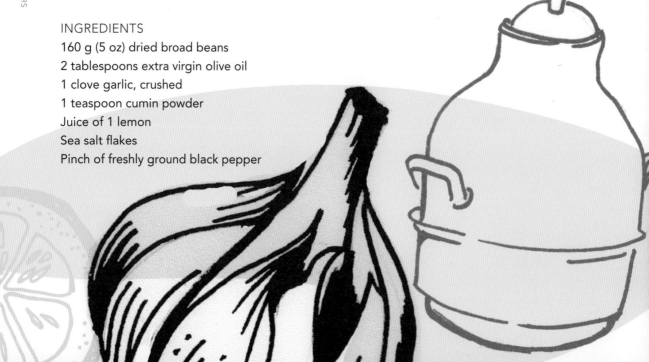

• Cover the beans in water and leave to soak overnight. Then drain and place in a large saucepan with plenty of fresh water. Bring to the boil, then simmer until tender. This may take 5–6 hours.

• Allow to cool slightly, then remove the skins by squeezing out the flesh of each bean and mash the flesh. If you don't want to go to the trouble of peeling the beans, you can purée the beans and skins together until you achieve a smooth consistency.

• Add the oil, garlic, cumin, and lemon juice. Season with salt and pepper and taste to check the balance of flavors, adjusting if necessary.

VARIATION

For a heartier *fuul medammis* you could add ½ small tomato, ½ small onion, and ½ small Lebanese cucumber, all very finely diced. Some people like to mash a boiled egg and some feta into the beans too. If adding any or all of these, check the flavor and add more garlic, oil, lemon juice, cumin, or salt as required.

'Eggah | Omelet with Grana Padano

Typically eaten at breakfast, this dish is similar to a Western omelet. The parsley gives it a dominant fresh flavor that is wonderful first thing in the morning, and helps to balance the more robust egg and fried onion. The beauty of this dish is the ease with which you can accommodate people: the ingredients are simple and few, so there are no difficulties in adjusting the quantities to suit the number of people eating. This would be a great dish to keep in mind for a very quick and easy midweek lunch or dinner. It could also be served sliced as part of a mezze platter, which is really useful when you have vegetarians among your party.

Serves: 1

INGREDIENTS
28 g (1 oz) butter
½ small onion, chopped
Small bunch flat-leaf parsley, finely chopped
2 teaspoons flour
2 eggs
Sea salt and freshly ground black pepper
2 thin slices Grana Padano or Parmesan

• Melt half the butter in a small frying pan over low heat, add the onion, and fry for 5 minutes until caramelized.

• Add the parsley and flour, and stir for 1–2 minutes. In the meantime, beat the eggs in a bowl and season with salt and pepper. Add the onion and parsley mixture to the eggs and stir well to combine.

• Heat the remaining butter in a frying pan; when it is bubbling, add the egg mixture, spreading it over the pan. Cook until the bottom is golden.

• Place the cheese in the center of the omelet and fold over. Cook each side for a further minute. Serve hot with fresh Lebanese flatbread or pita bread.

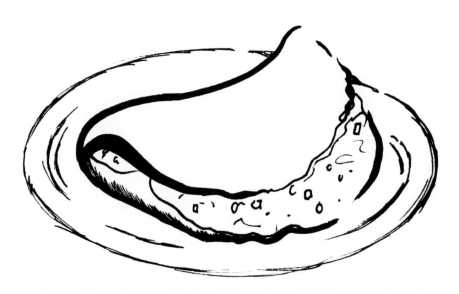

Koshari | Egyptian Khichdi

This meal is very popular and is found in many restaurants, cafés, and takeaway places in Egypt. The combination of rice, pasta, and lentils results in a carbohydrate-loaded vegetarian dish, which is quite unusual.

It is simple to make, because each component is independently prepared and then the dish easily assembled. When I was in Egypt filming the cooking show *The Taste, Middle East*, I was keen to try koshari at the first opportunity. I love that it is a 'fast food' and is sold next to KFC and hot chips in the food courts. Like everyone around me, I really enjoyed eating this, with its little containers of sauce and stock. Next to me a father and son were enjoying the same dish with a serving of chicken livers on top. There is no end to the variations!

Serves: 6

INGREDIENTS
100 g (3½ oz) brown lentils, washed and drained
200 g (7 oz) white long-grain rice
120 g (4 oz) boiled or canned chickpeas
1 cup raw macaroni pasta

Rich tomato sauce
1 tablespoon olive oil
1 medium onion, finely chopped
2 cloves garlic, crushed
1½ cups (375 ml) tomato sauce or passata
¼ teaspoon chili powder (optional)
½ teaspoon ground cumin
¼ teaspoon salt
⅛ teaspoon ground black pepper
1 cup (250 ml) water

Onion garnish
¼ cup (60 ml) vegetable oil
2 large onions, sliced

Special sauce
1 tablespoon oil
1–2 cloves garlic, crushed
1 teaspoon ground coriander
¼ cup (60 ml) white vinegar
Sea salt and freshly ground black pepper
250 ml (1 cup) water

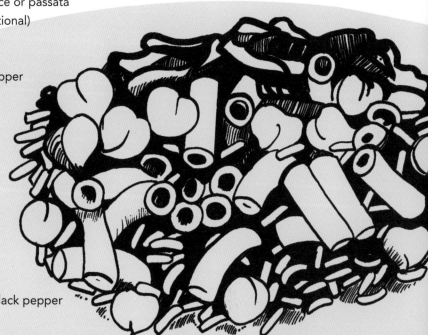

- Begin by making the special sauce. In a small saucepan, heat the oil over medium heat, then add the garlic and fry for 2 minutes. Add the coriander, vinegar, and a sprinkling of salt and pepper. Add the water, bring to the boil, then remove and pour into a serving dish. Adjust the seasoning as necessary.

- To cook the lentils, put them into a pan with 2 cups (500 ml) of water and bring to a boil. Simmer over medium heat for 20 minutes then drain.

- Replace the lentils in the pan. Add 2 cups (500 ml) of fresh water and all the rice. Cover, bring to a boil, then simmer for 20 minutes or until the rice is soft.

- While the lentils and rice are cooking, prepare the rich tomato sauce. Heat the oil in a pan and fry the onion and garlic until golden brown. Add the tomato sauce or passata, chili powder, cumin, salt, and pepper. Add the water and bring to the boil, then lower the heat and simmer for 20–25 minutes until the sauce has reduced and thickened.

- Prepare the onion garnish. Heat the oil in a saucepan over medium heat and add the sliced onion. Fry for 20–25 minutes or until the onion is soft and caramelized. Set aside.

- Begin to cook the macaroni at around the same time that you cook the rice. Fill a separate pan with water and a sprinkle of salt, and bring to a boil. Add the macaroni to the boiling water and cook until tender, according to packet directions, then drain.

- Combine the lentils, rice, macaroni, and sauces. Layer the components as follows: 1st layer—rice and lentils; 2nd layer—macaroni; 3rd layer—chickpeas; 4th layer—rich tomato sauce; 5th layer—small amount of special sauce; 6th layer—onion garnish.

- Put the dish directly onto the table and serve with a small jug of special sauce.

COOK'S TIP
This dish can be assembled and kept in a warm oven for 10–15 minutes until required.

Ta'miya | Falafel

Falafel is another popular Egyptian dish that is traditionally eaten for breakfast. The patties are made of fried broad (fava) beans that have been soaked overnight, peeled, and blended to a paste (in other parts of the Arab world, it is more often made using a mix of fava beans and chickpeas). Today, you can buy packaged 'falafel mixes,' in dried and frozen versions, but freshly made falafel tastes far better. I can recall throwing a basket containing coins over the balcony of my uncle's place in Egypt to a street vendor below, who was walking down the street and yelling that he had fresh falafel. He would take the money out of the basket and place a cone (made out of newspaper) full of fresh falafel in its place. We would then hoist the basket up and sit down to breakfast. Very quick and yummy!

   Falafel is sometimes served in sandwiches and in pita, and it is often accompanied with *baba ghanoug* (page 39) or *tahina* (page 36). This recipe makes a large quantity but it can easily be frozen and then thawed out before the shaping and frying stages.

Makes: 10–12

INGREDIENTS
500 g (1 lb) dried broad beans
3 tablespoons coriander seeds
2 onions or 1 bunch spring onions, chopped
2 large cloves garlic, crushed
1 bunch parsley, finely chopped
1 leek, washed thoroughly
2–3 tablespoons ground cumin
2–3 tablespoons ground coriander
1 tablespoon baking powder
Salt and pepper, to taste
Vegetable oil, for deep-frying

• Soak the beans in water for 24 hours or more to soften them. Drain and skin them, by slitting the skin of each one and popping out the flesh. Place in a food processor and blend briefly.

• Roast the coriander seeds by placing them in a small pan and dry-frying them for a few minutes until fragrant. Allow to cool, then crush lightly.

• Add the onion, garlic, parsley, leek, cumin, ground coriander, coriander seeds, baking powder, and salt and pepper to taste. Blend to a smooth paste, then leave to rest for at least 30 minutes.

• Take a tablespoon of the mixture and shape it into a ball about the size of a walnut shell. Place it on a chopping board or large plate and press to flatten it slightly. Repeat until you have used all the mixture. Leave the flattened balls to rest for another 15 minutes.

• Heat some oil in a deep fryer until hot, then fry the falafel in batches until they become a dark, rich, golden-brown color. Remove and drain on paper towel. Serve hot.

Sambousa bi-l-gibna | Ricotta Triangles

These crispy triangles are a perfect finger food and they always go down well at parties. They can be made in advance and baked just before serving. Filo pastry can be found in many supermarkets today, as well as in delicatessens, in both fresh and frozen form. If you buy frozen pastry, simply leave it to thaw while still sealed in the plastic wrapping.

In this recipe the pastry triangles are filled with ricotta cheese to make a delicious vegetarian dish, but they can also be filled with minced meat (*sambousa bi-l-lahma*, page 54). If you can't source the marinated Persian feta, use a marinated Greek feta.

Makes: 21–24

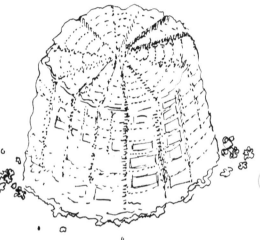

INGREDIENTS
1 tablespoon ghee or butter, plus some for brushing
½ onion, finely chopped
500 g (1 lb) full-cream ricotta cheese
100 g (3½ oz) marinated Persian feta cheese, crumbled
½ bunch flat-leaf parsley leaves, finely chopped
¼ cup (60 ml) olive oil
Pinch salt and pepper
375 g (12 oz) filo pastry

• Preheat the oven to 180°C (350°F/Gas mark 4). Melt the butter in a frying pan, add the onion, and cook for 5 minutes or until slightly caramelized.

• In a bowl, combine the ricotta, feta, parsley, fried onion, and oil. Season to taste with salt and pepper (but remember that the feta is salty).

• Remove all the pastry from the packet and, working quickly, cut the sheets in half. Take one of the top sheets (cover the remaining sheets with a clean damp tea towel to keep them from drying out), brush it with melted butter, and fold it in half lengthways.

• Place a tablespoon of the ricotta mixture at the bottom left corner of the pastry strip, making a triangular shape with the mixture. Fold up the bottom left corner, lifting up the mixture and moving it toward the right, making a triangle shape with the pastry as you cover the filling. Now fold the triangle containing the filling over to the right. Continue folding in this manner until all the pastry is used up.

• Repeat the process until you have used all the filling and pastry. Brush the top of each triangle with butter and place on a lightly greased tray, folded side down. Bake for 20–25 minutes until golden brown. Serve immediately.

Sambousa bi-l-lahma | Mince Triangles

This is a meaty alternative to the vegetarian ricotta triangles, and uses the same folding method. The meat filling can easily be made in advance and the triangles assembled on the day of baking. If using filling that has been frozen, make sure it has thawed to room temperature before using. Don't ever be tempted to use hot filling—this will ruin the pastry and make folding it into shape nearly impossible (yes, I have made this mistake before).

Makes: 21–24

INGREDIENTS
1 tablespoon olive oil
1 onion, finely chopped
300 g (10½ oz) minced beef
Salt and pepper, to taste
1 cup (250 ml) water
375g (12 oz) filo pastry
Ghee or melted butter for brushing

• Preheat the oven to 180°C (350 °F/Gas mark 4). Heat the oil in a pan, add the onion and meat, and fry until browned. Add some salt and pepper, then pour in the water and allow to simmer, stirring occasionally, until the liquid has evaporated. Remove from heat and cool.

• Remove all the pastry from the packets and, working quickly, cut the sheets in half. Take one of the top sheets (cover the remaining sheets with a clean damp tea towel to keep them from drying out), brush it with melted butter, and fold it in half lengthways.

• Place a tablespoon of the beef mixture on the left hand edge. Fold as for Ricotta Triangles (page 53). Repeat the process until you have used all the filling.

• Brush the top of each triangle with butter and place on a greased tray, folded side down. Bake for 20–25 minutes until golden brown. Serve immediately.

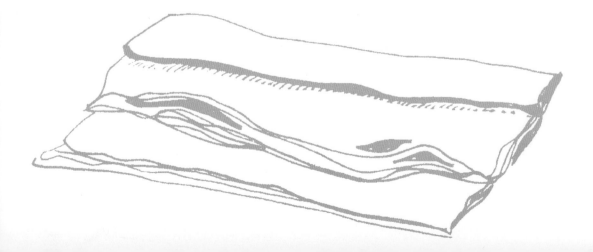

Hawawshi | Spiced-mince Pita Parcels

Hawawshi is a form of bread filled with spiced minced meat and baked. In Egypt the bread is traditionally made fresh, but at home I just use pita or Lebanese bread. We often eat this for a Sunday lunch—I love the buttery, crunchy bread and the delicate onion flavor of the mince. As with most recipes, it is easy to make this recipe your own by adding whatever flavors you prefer (or using whatever you have in the fridge). Chopped mushroom, parsley, capsicum, chili, and cayenne pepper all work well in *hawawshi*.

My mum used to wrap the bread up in newspaper but I think it is better to use butchers' paper as there is no ink-burning smell and less of a hygiene risk! You can also use foil or baking parchment, but if so, you may need to open the parcel and cook for a further 5 minutes to make the bread crisper, as the foil or parchment will trap moisture, while the butchers' paper will absorb it.

Makes: 5

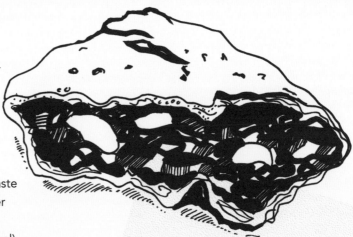

INGREDIENTS
1 kg (2¼ lb) minced beef
2–3 large onions, finely chopped
2 cloves garlic, crushed
2 tomatoes chopped (optional)
¼ red capsicum, or pepper
¼ green capsicum, or pepper
¼ yellow capsicum, or pepper
1 teaspoon salt and pepper, or to taste
1½ tablespoons mixed spice powder
1 teaspoon allspice or nutmeg
1½ teaspoons ground cumin (optional)
1 tablespoon pomegranate molasses (optional)
5 Lebanese or pita breads
Butter, for brushing

- Preheat the oven to 200°C (400°F/Gas mark 6). Combine all the ingredients except the bread in a food processor and blend well.

- Split open each bread by cutting three-quarters of the way down one edge. Divide the meat mixture evenly between the breads. Taking each bread in turn, spread the mixture around one half of the inner surfaces, evenly and almost to the edge. Place small dots of butter on the surface of the meat, and then close the bread. Brush both sides of the bread with melted butter.

- Wrap each bread in butchers' paper so it is completely enclosed. Cook for 30–40 minutes or until the meat is cooked and the bread is golden brown and crunchy.

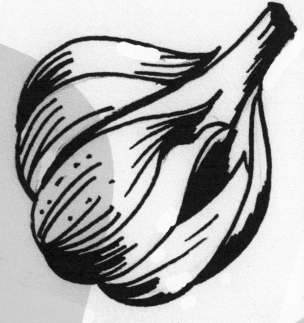

Bastirma bi-l-beid | Fenugreek-spiced Cured Beef and Egg

Bastirma is cured beef that has been spiced with fenugreek. It is super-salty and at home we had this with fried eggs, sliced tomato, and onions, and Lebanese or pita bread. It is incredibly simple, which makes it great for a quick and easy meal. For a variation you could substitute slices of cooked *kofta* (page 98) or chorizo for the *bastirma* if you wish.

Serves: 1–2

INGREDIENTS
2–3 slices of bastirma
2 eggs
Freshly ground black pepper

- For each person, fry a slice or two of bastirma broken into pieces.
- When crispy, add a couple of eggs and cook to your liking—scrambled, fried, or omelet style.
- Add some pepper and serve with fresh Lebanese bread and salad.

Kobeba | Bulgur and Meat Loaf

Kobeba is like a meat loaf, but it is made using bulgur wheat and mince, with some spiced mince in the center. In Lebanon it is known as *kibbeh* and eaten as part of mezze. My dad didn't eat this growing up, so clearly it is not a dish that is eaten all over Egypt. We ate this as a main meal with salad at home, but it is generally served as an appetizer in Egypt. This can be fried rather than oven-baked, if preferred.

Serves: 4–6

INGREDIENTS
500 g (1 lb) fine brown bulgur wheat
2–3 large onions, cut into quarters
500 g (1 lb) lean ground beef
2 teaspoons salt
½ –1 teaspoon freshly ground black pepper
1½ teaspoons mace or nutmeg
2 teaspoons cinnamon

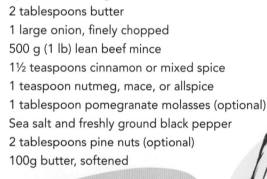

Spiced meat filling
2 tablespoons butter
1 large onion, finely chopped
500 g (1 lb) lean beef mince
1½ teaspoons cinnamon or mixed spice
1 teaspoon nutmeg, mace, or allspice
1 tablespoon pomegranate molasses (optional)
Sea salt and freshly ground black pepper
2 tablespoons pine nuts (optional)
100g butter, softened

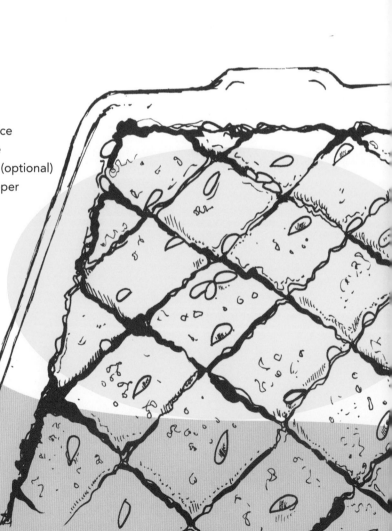

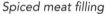

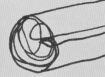

- Boil some water in a kettle. Place the bulgur wheat in a large bowl and cover it with the boiled water. Leave for 1–2 hours or until the water has been absorbed—the wheat should be soft and have doubled in volume. Remove any excess water by straining with a sieve and place the wheat into a large bowl.

- Make the spiced meat filling. In a large pan, melt the butter and fry the onion for 2 minutes until golden. Add the meat and brown over a medium heat. Add the spices, pomegranate molasses, and season to taste. Add 1 to 2 cups (250–500 ml) water to cover the meat. Bring to the boil on high heat, then simmer until all the liquid has evaporated.

- Add the pine nuts and cook for a further 2 minutes.

- While the spiced mixture is simmering, use a meat mincer to mince together the ground beef, cooked bulgur, and onion quarters (if you don't have a mincer, use a food processor to mince to a fine paste). Collect the combined mixture into a bowl and add the salt, pepper, mace, and cinnamon. Remove and set aside.

- Preheat the oven to 180°C (350°F/Gas mark 4). Grease a 30 by 25 cm (12 by 10 in) baking dish. Place half the bulgur mixture into the dish and flatten using the palm of your hand. Spread the spiced mince over the base. Use the remaining bulgur mixture to cover the meat. You may need to wet your hands to flatten the bulgur for the top layer.

- Cut the kobeba into squares. Place a few small dollops of butter on top, then place in the oven and bake for 30–40 minutes until the top is golden brown.

VARIATION

An alternative way of serving *kobeba* is to make it into cocoon shapes. Take ¼ of a cup of the bulgur mix, flatten it, then use your palm to form a cup shape. Fill with the meat stuffing, then carefully close to enclose the filling. Repeat until all the bulgur mix is used. Keep these in the fridge until required, then deep-fry them in batches just before serving.

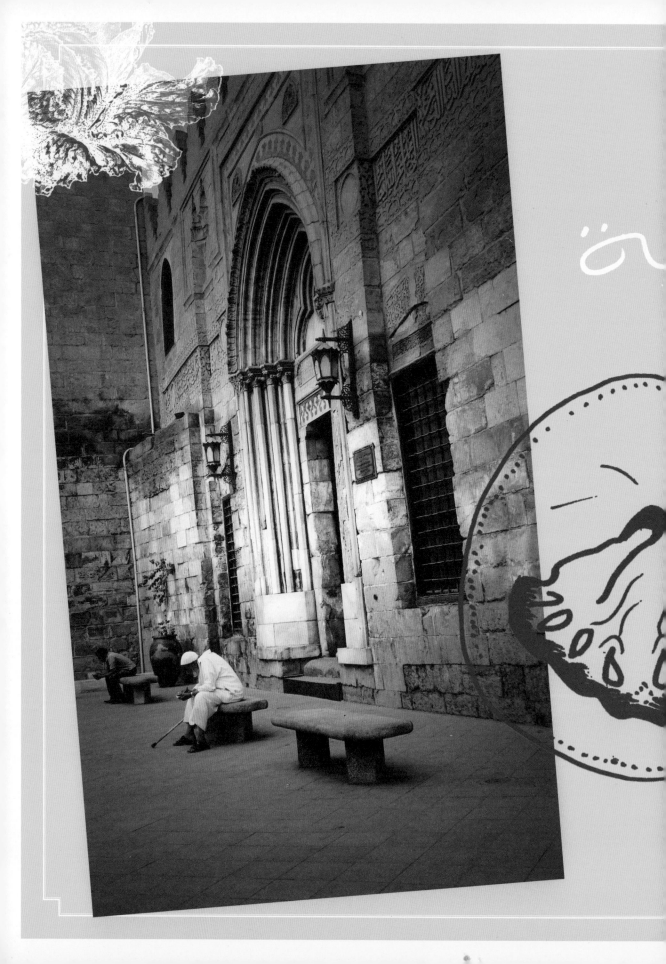

MAIN COURSES

MAIN COURSES

The main meal of the day (our evening meal) is precious to me, a time when we can all sit down together and ask each other about our day. No rushing to get ready for school or work or catching the train on time. We switch the television off and put our phones aside. It's a peaceful time to share a meal together. (Admittedly, I am still waiting for the peaceful part, as in our house there is still the rush to get food to the table before the children hit the hungry stage and emotional meltdowns ensue.)

The meals in this section are filling and wholesome in a day and age when fast food and processed meals are so readily available and popular. Knowing what goes into the food we eat and where that food comes from is so important and yet many kids grow up with narrow tastes and little or no desire to taste and experiment with food. I encourage my kids to walk around the garden and watch the plants grow, to water the plants, and to pick from them when the fruits of our labor are ripe. I love them to be in the kitchen and to cook with me, and to get dirty, whether in the garden, planting, or mixing dough. I hope to pass on to them the joy I have experienced in preparing the dishes I included in this section.

Lahma bi-l-zabadi | Lamb and Yogurt

Braised meat is lovely in the cooler months, because it is often hearty and rich in flavor while also very simple and easy to prepare. This dish, along with the two that follow—Braised Beef Cubes (page 65) and Braised Beef in Passata (page 66)—are very cost effective because the cheaper cuts of meat are ideal; they become very tender with long, slow cooking. You can cook these in a heavy-based pan, but a slow cooker works well here, because these are 'set and forget' meals: set up the ingredients in the morning, forget about the dish all day, then come home to a beautifully cooked meal that's ready to eat.

This is not a traditional Egyptian dish. It's loosely based on a Lebanese meat dish cooked in yogurt that I once tried when having lunch with a family friend, over a decade ago. My memories of it are vague except for the fact that it was delicious. Since it was not a meal I ever had at home, or in any Egyptian household, I invented my own version as a great way of using my homemade yogurt (page 16). The first time I served it to my family I was unsure they would like it, but as it turned out, they enjoyed this as much as I did.

Serves: 4

INGREDIENTS
1 tablespoon vegetable oil
1 large onion, finely chopped
3 cloves garlic, crushed
1 kg (2¼ lb) lamb, cut into 2 cm (¾ inch) cubes
2 large tomatoes, diced
1 teaspoon vegetable stock powder
¼ teaspoon ground cinnamon
¼ teaspoon ground black pepper
1 teaspoon dried thyme
1 bay leaf
2 cups (500 ml) natural yogurt
2 tablespoons cornstarch

- Heat a little oil in a heavy-based pan over medium heat. Fry the onion for 2 minutes, then add the garlic and fry for a further minute.

- Add the lamb and cook for a further 10 minutes, allowing the meat to brown.

- Add the tomatoes along with the vegetable stock powder, cinnamon, and pepper.

- Stir all the ingredients and leave them to bubble gently for a few minutes, then add the thyme, bay leaf, and yogurt.

- Dissolve the cornstarch in 2 tablespoons of water and add to the pan. Stir well, then cover and leave to cook for 6 hours at a very low heat, or in a slow cooker. Serve over rice.

Lahma bi-l-shorba |
Braised Beef Cubes

This dish doesn't have much in the way of ingredients, as most of the flavor comes from the braised meat itself, so you don't want it to be disguised by other strong flavors. If using beef rump, cook it more slowly and for longer than if you are using beef blade. The use of a pressure cooker cuts down the cooking time considerably and will result in lovely, tender meat. I have also made this in a slow cooker, browning the meat and adding 1½ cups (375 ml) water, then cooking on the fastest setting for about 2 hours. For a quick finish, serve with some fresh Lebanese or pita bread and steamed vegetables or a salad.

Serves: 4

INGREDIENTS
1 tablespoon butter
3–4 cloves garlic, crushed
1 kg (2¼ lb) beef cut into 2 cm (¾ inch) cubes
1 bay leaf
Sea salt and freshly ground black pepper

• In a large heavy-based pan or pressure cooker, melt the butter and fry the garlic over a medium heat for 2 minutes until golden in color. Do not allow it to brown.

• Add the beef and cook over a high heat until well browned. Do not worry if the base of the saucepan browns as this will add color and flavor to the liquid. Add the bay leaf and salt and pepper to taste. Cook for a further 2 minutes.

• Add enough water to cover the meat, then cover and cook on a low heat for 60 minutes (15–20 minutes if using a pressure cooker) until the meat is tender and cooked.

> **COOK'S TIP**
> Check the dish 15 minutes before the end of the cooking time; if there is too much liquid, add a little cornstarch mixed with water to thicken the sauce.

Lahma bi-l-dem'a | Braised Beef in Passata

At home we made our own tomato sauce. It was a family affair that took an entire day, but it resulted in enough bottled sauce to last a year. This dish was a great excuse for using it, but for those without the equipment, time, or inclination to make their own tomato sauce, the shop-bought version—or passata—is absolutely fine here. I have added basil as an option because we used it in our homemade sauce to add a delicate flavor, but it can be omitted without any significant loss of taste.

Serves: 4

INGREDIENTS
1 tablespoon ghee
1 onion, finely chopped
2 cloves garlic, crushed
1 kg (2¼ lb) chuck steak, cut into 2 cm (¾ inch) cubes
½ teaspoon mace or allspice
2 cups (500 ml) tomato sauce or passata
Sea salt and freshly ground black pepper
1 cup (250 ml) beef stock
½ teaspoon dried basil (optional)

• In a large heavy-based saucepan or pressure cooker, melt the ghee and fry the onion and garlic over a medium heat for 2 minutes until golden in color.

• Add the meat and cook over a high heat until browned. Add the mace or allspice. Cook for a further 2 minutes.

• Add the tomato sauce or passata and just enough water to cover the meat. Season with salt and pepper, then cover and cook on low heat for 1½ hours (15–20 minutes if using a pressure cooker), until the meat is cooked and tender. Serve over white rice.

Batatis bi-l-dem'a | Tender Beef and Potato Stew

This dish brings back memories of loitering by the kitchen waiting for the potatoes to be cooked, so that I could nibble on a few, not unlike the way seagulls hover around for leftovers at the beach. I am sure my kids will do this when they are older too.

This is a carbohydrate-loaded dish as the potato is served over rice, but it is very tasty and really lovely as a warm winter meal. It can't be frozen, because the cooked potatoes do not freeze well and tend to disintegrate upon thawing, but it can be stored in the fridge for several days. I have used soy sauce for saltiness here and it adds a little flavor, but if you prefer, this can be omitted or replaced with sea salt to taste.

Serves: 4

INGREDIENTS
2 tablespoons oil, plus oil for frying
1 large onion, chopped
1 kg (2¼ lb) gravy or shin beef, cut into 4–6 large pieces
140 g (5 oz) thickened tomato paste
1½ cups (375 ml) tomato sauce or passata
1 tablespoon soy sauce
½ teaspoon freshly ground black pepper
½ teaspoon mixed spice
½ teaspoon allspice
Chili powder, to taste (optional)
1 kg (2¼ lb) potatoes

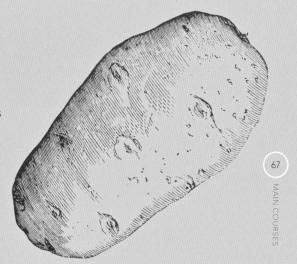

• Heat 2 tablespoons oil in a pressure cooker or heavy-based pot. Fry the onion and beef until browned.

• Add the tomato paste and sauce, along with the soy sauce, seasoning, and spice. Cook for a further 2 minutes.

• Add 1½ cups (375 ml) of water. Bring to the boil, then reduce the heat, cover, and simmer for 1½ hours or until the meat is tender.

• In the meantime, peel, wash, and dry the potatoes, then cut them into 2.5 cm (1 inch) cubes.

• Heat some oil in a deep-fryer and fry the potatoes in batches until golden, then remove and drain on paper towel. Alternatively, shallow-fry the potatoes in a large frying pan.

• When the meat is tender, add the fried potatoes and cook for a further 2 minutes. Remove from heat and serve with rice and salad.

COOK'S TIP
You can reduce the cooking time by cutting the meat into 2 cm (¾ inch) cubes, which need to be simmered for only 45 minutes.

Fasolya tabikh | One-pot Beef and Bean Stew

The simple heart of this recipe—stewing meat in vegetables and tomatoes—formed the basis of many of the meals I ate at home. The word *tabikh* refers to any dish that is cooked, but it may hark back to a remarkable collection of recipes from ninth-century Baghdad, entitled *Kitab al-tabikh* (The Book of Recipes). Baghdad was then the wealthiest city in the world, and at the center of of its courtly cuisine were rich and complex stews such as this one. The stews were often served with rice that had been cooked in the *tannuur* (tandoori oven) overnight with the meat and spices, but in my home they were always eaten with simple boiled rice or rice with vermicelli (page 22).

The dish can be made in a pressure cooker if you have one; this will reduce the cooking time by about half while still producing tender meat.

Serves: 4

INGREDIENTS
1 tablespoon ghee or butter
1 large onion, chopped
500 g (1 lb) shin beef or topside, cut into 10–12 rough chunks
1 teaspoon ground pepper
1 teaspoon ground allspice
1 teaspoon mixed spice
400 g (14 oz) green beans
2 carrots, finely chopped (optional)
140 g (5 oz) thickened tomato paste
1½ cups (375 ml) tomato sauce or passata

- In a heavy-based pan or pressure cooker, melt the ghee or butter over medium heat and fry the onion until soft and caramelized.

- Add the meat and spices, stir, and allow to cook until the beef chunks are browned.

- While the meat is cooking, top and tail the green beans and cut into 2cm (¾ inch) segments. Peel and finely chop the carrots. When the meat has browned, add the beans and cook for 2 minutes.

- Add the tomato paste and sauce, along with enough water to cover the meat. Cover and cook at a simmer for 50–60 minutes or until the meat is cooked all the way through. Add the carrots and cook for a further 10 minutes. Serve with rice.

COOK'S TIP
You could use dried beans such as cannellini or black-eyed peas in place of the green beans here. These need only to be soaked overnight, then added to the meat and sauce to cook. If you want to increase the vegetable content, add 110g (4 oz) fresh peas and 90 g (3 oz) sweet corn along with the carrots.

Kofta bi-l-dem'a | Spicy Meatballs

This Egyptian version of meatballs includes cumin powder, which adds a new dimension to the traditional meatballs recipe without overpowering it. If you want to increase the vegetable content, you could add vegetables to the sauce during cooking—peas and carrots go well but anything would work. This is a great recipe to make ahead of time or make in double quantities and freeze (thaw out overnight in the fridge for best results).

Serves: 4

INGREDIENTS
500 g (1 lb) minced beef
1 medium onion, grated or finely chopped
1 clove garlic, crushed
¼ teaspoon sea salt
⅛ teaspoon freshly ground black pepper
½ teaspoon mixed spice or cinnamon
½ teaspoons cumin powder
1 tablespoon chopped flat-leaf parsley
Ghee or vegetable oil, for frying
2 tablespoons rice flour

Spicy tomato sauce
1 tablespoon ghee or butter
1 medium onion, finely chopped
2 cloves garlic, crushed
1½ cups (375 ml) tomato paste or passata
⅛ teaspoon ground pepper
¼ teaspoon salt
½ teaspoon mixed spice powder
½ teaspoon ground allspice
1 tablespoon chopped basil
½ teaspoon cayenne pepper or chili powder (optional)

• Place all the ingredients for the meatballs in a bowl. Using your hands, combine together really well. Take a tablespoon of the mixture and roll into a ball about the size of a walnut. Place the meatball on a large plate. Repeat the process until all of the meat mixture has been used.

• Make the tomato sauce. Melt the butter or ghee in a large saucepan over a medium heat and add the onion and garlic. Cook for 2 minutes, then add the tomato paste or passata and 1 cup (250 ml) water. Add the pepper, salt, mixed spice, allspice, basil, and cayenne pepper or chili powder, and bring to the boil. Reduce to a simmer while you cook the meatballs.

• Heat the butter or ghee in a frying pan and fry the meatballs—in batches if necessary—until browned all over. Alternatively, heat some oil in a deep fryer and deep-fry the meatballs until well browned, then remove and drain on paper towel.

• Add the meatballs to the sauce. The meatballs should be covered by the sauce; if not, add water as necessary.

• Cover and cook on a high heat for 10 minutes, then reduce to a medium heat for 15–20 minutes or until the meatballs are tender. If the tomato sauce has not reduced or is too watery, add the rice flour to thicken before serving. Serve over rice.

COOK'S TIP

Leftover roast vegetables make a wonderful thickener in place of rice flour in this recipe, because they bring a subtle roasted flavor to the dish. Simply purée all the leftover vegetables (I use anything from garlic and onion to pumpkin, potato, zucchini, eggplant, and even beetroot.) Add a little water to help the blending process. Use around 1 cup (250 ml) of the purée in place of the water in this recipe. If it is too thick, add a little more water until it reaches a sauce-like consistency.

'Akkawi | Slow-cooked Oxtail

Oxtail is literally the tail of a cow that has been skinned and cut into portions—which doesn't sound very appealing, but when cooked, the meat is so incredibly tender it just melts in your mouth. It is not a very popular cut of meat, perhaps because it is relatively unknown in some countries. The best place to find this is in a large produce market or good butcher; if neither stock oxtails, they may be willing to order them in for you.

Slow-cooked oxtail is a simple dish with a delicate flavor and the stock it produces is delicious. The meat is cooked in plenty of water with vegetables and seasoning, and after the cooked meat has been removed, the stock can be reduced, cooled, and refrigerated overnight (allowing the fats to solidify for easy removal). The resulting stock is light but full of flavor, and it can be used to add a meaty zest to other dishes such as *molokhiya* (page 120) or *fatta* (page 118).

Serves: 4

INGREDIENTS
1 oxtail, cut into 7 or 8 pieces
1 onion, peeled and with a cross cut into the top
Sea salt and freshly ground black pepper
1 bay leaf
1 tablespoon butter or ghee

• Place 6 cups (1½ liters) of water in a heavy-based pan and bring to the boil.

• Add the oxtail pieces along with the onion, salt, pepper, and bay leaf. Cover and cook gently on low heat for 2 hours or until the meat is tender and separates from the bone. While the meat is cooking, remove any foam or impurities as they rise to the surface.

• When the meat is cooked, remove it from the stock and set aside. Strain the stock, discard the vegetables, and leave to cool. The stock can then be refrigerated or frozen for use in other dishes.

• Melt the butter or ghee in a frying pan and fry the oxtail, turning it several times, until browned on the surface. Serve with *molokhiya* (page 120), rice, and salad.

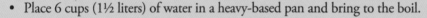

VARIATION
As an alternative to finishing the oxtail by frying, try placing the cooked meat in a baking tray with some vegetables—I sometimes add 3 or 4 sliced potatoes, 1 or 2 sliced onions, and a couple of sliced tomatoes. Stir through 100g (3½ oz) thickened tomato paste dissolved in 2 cups (500 ml) of water (or use 2 cups/500 ml tomato sauce or passata) and then bake it in the oven at 180°C (350°F/Gas mark 4) for 40 minutes or until the vegetables are tender.

Mahshi wara' 'enab | Stuffed Vine Leaves

Serves: 2

INGREDIENTS

250 g (½ lb) minced beef
1 onion, finely chopped
½ cup flat-leaf parsley, finely
   chopped
100 g (3½ oz) white rice
½ teaspoon mace or mixed spice
Salt and pepper, to taste
250 g (½ lb) fresh vine leaves,
   plus extra for pan lining, or
   200 g (7 oz) canned leaves
1–2 cups (250–500 ml) chicken or
   beef stock
3 tablespoons lemon juice
1 tablespoon olive oil

Mint yogurt sauce
½ cup (125 g) Greek-style yogurt
Handful of fresh mint, very finely
   sliced
Juice of ½ lemon
50 g (1¾ oz) marinated feta
   cheese, crumbled

Stuffed Vine Leaves are always served at special occasions, such as Christmas. The time and effort required to make this dish is well worth it—my dad often says that this is the best food in the world! Needless to say, because it was my dad's favorite, my mum would prepare it often. *Mahshi wara' 'enab* is famous in Lebanon, Syria, Jordan, Palestine, Egypt, and Iraq, but the mint seasoning makes the dish classically Lebanese. In Egypt, unlike some other countries, it is eaten hot and as part of the main meal, rather than as an appetizer. The Egyptian version is also very small, comparatively speaking, and usually has a certain mixture (*khaltat wara' 'enab*) made of rice, onions, and parsley as a stuffing.

Fresh vine leaves are the best form to use if possible—if you have access to a grape vine, select the younger, tender leaves. Choose leaves that are large but a lighter green than the older ones. I pick mine when I need them so they are as fresh as possible, but if you are not using them immediately you can freeze the leaves and use them later (simply thaw them out well and blanch them in boiling water as for freshly picked leaves). Vine leaves can also be bought canned, soaked in brine, from some supermarkets and delicatessens.

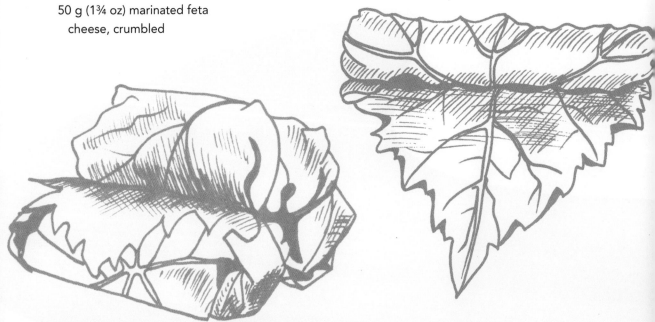

- Combine the ingredients for the mint yogurt sauce and set aside.

- In a bowl, combine the meat, onion, parsley, rice, mace, salt, and pepper.

- If you are using fresh vine leaves, bring plenty of water to the boil in a large pan and blanch in batches until they change from bright green to a khaki color. Set aside. If you are using canned vine leaves, soak them in water and drain 2 or 3 times to remove excess salt.

- Carefully separate all the vine leaves. Place each leaf shiny-side down, with its stem toward you. Put 1 teaspoon of the stuffing near the bottom of the leaf or stem, then fold the leaf: start by folding from the bottom up, then fold in the 2 sides to cover the filling, and complete by rolling tightly toward the tip of the leaf. Repeat the process until you have used all the stuffing.

- If you are using fresh leaves, line a pan with a few of them to stop the stuffed leaves from sticking. These leaves will not be eaten, so older leaves are fine. Place the vine rolls in the pan (folded-edge down) and tightly packed together. Cover with several of the remaining vine leaves. (When my mother was cooking this, she would wrap any leftover stuffing in foil and place it on top to cook.) Cover the rolls completely with stock and add the lemon juice and oil. Cook for 25–30 minutes or until the rice and the leaves are tender and the liquid has evaporated. Serve with the mint yogurt sauce.

Mahshi | Mixed Stuffed Vegetables in Rich Tomato Sauce

Mahshi, which can be used to refer to any kind of stuffed vegetables, is loved by families all over the Mediterranean. It is always one of the most important dishes in dinner gatherings. The stuffing for this recipe can be used with zucchini, Lebanese eggplant, and capsicum (bell peppers).

Serves: 4

INGREDIENTS
1½–2 kg (3–4½ lb) mixed vegetables such as zucchini, eggplant, and capsicum (bell peppers)
3 cups (750 ml) tomato sauce or passata
4 cups (1 liter) beef stock

Stuffing
500 g (1 lb) minced or ground beef
I teaspoon mixed spice powder
2 teaspoons oil, ghee, or melted butter (optional)
300 g (10½ oz) white short-grain rice
½ cup (125 ml) tomato sauce or passata
1 teaspoon mixed spice powder
½ teaspoon allspice powder
1½ teaspoon sea salt
½ teaspoon ground black pepper
2 medium onions, finely chopped or minced
1 bunch flat-leaf parsley, finely chopped

> **COOK'S TIP**
> If you are left with any extra mince after stuffing the vegetables, wrap it in foil and place it on top of the vegetables during the last stage of cooking.

- Combine all the stuffing ingredients together in a bowl and mix well.

- Halve the eggplant and zucchini and use a vegetable corer (this is known as a *ma'wara* in Arabic) to remove and discard the flesh, leaving a 1 cm (½ inch) border. Do not puncture the ends. Cut the tops off any bell peppers and clean out the inside.

- Stuff the vegetables with the meat mixture, making sure it is firmly packed, but be careful not to push the stuffing through the vegetable ends. Pack the vegetables into a large pan with the open ends facing upward.

- Pour the tomato sauce and stock over the vegetables. Add warm water to the pan until it comes up to the height of the vegetables. Bring to the boil over a high heat, then reduce to a medium heat and cook for 75–90 minutes or until the vegetables are tender and the rice is well cooked. Add boiling water to the pan during cooking if needed.

- Arrange the stuffed vegetables on a serving platter and serve while hot.

Mahshi kromb | Cabbage Rolls with Dill

Cabbage rolls use the same stuffing as for the stuffed vegetables on page 76, but the cabbage is prepared slightly differently. The cabbage is also married up with dill in this recipe and with the hint of cumin it tastes marvelous.

Serves: 6

INGREDIENTS
1 whole cabbage
1 tablespoon cumin seeds
1 tablespoon salt
3 cups (750 ml) tomato sauce
  or passata
4 cups (1 liter) salt-reduced beef
  stock

Stuffing
1 teaspoon mixed spice powder
½ teaspoon allspice powder
1½ teaspoons salt
½ teaspoon ground black pepper
300 g (10½ oz) white short-grain
  rice
2 medium onions, finely chopped
  or minced
1 bunch flat-leaf parsley, finely
  chopped
500 g (1 lb) beef, minced or
  ground
1 teaspoon chopped dill

• Combine all the stuffing ingredients together in a bowl and mix well.

• Separate the leaves of the cabbage. Fill a large pot with water and bring to the boil over a high heat. Add the cumin and salt.

• Add the cabbage leaves to the water, in batches as large as your pan will allow. Cook until the leaves soften (about 5 minutes), then remove them from the water and set aside until all the leaves have been cooked.

• Remove the outer leaves of the cabbage, cut the larger leaves in half, and remove any hard core from every leaf. Keep the outer leaves for use later.

• To fill, lay a leaf on a chopping board and spread it out fully. Place a line of stuffing at the center, leaving a 1 cm (½ inch) border. Fold in the bottom end, over the meat, tuck in the sides, and then roll to cover the stuffing. Cut off any excess. Repeat the process until all of the stuffing or leaves have been used.

• Using the cabbage offcuts, layer the base of a pan with cabbage leaves. Place each of the cabbage rolls into the pot with the folded-edge down, arranging them side by side in a layer. Build up the layers as necessary. When completed, place any leftover meat in foil and place it on top of the cabbage rolls.

• Add the tomato sauce or passata. Then add the beef stock, using as much as necessary to cover the rolls. (If they are still not covered, add water as required.) Place the pan over a high heat to bring to a boil, then reduce the heat and simmer for 50–60 minutes or until the meat and rice are cooked. Serve.

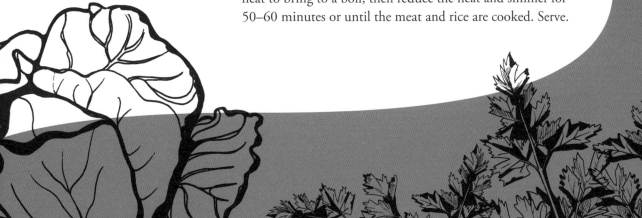

Kharshuf fi-l-forn | Roasted Artichoke in Red Pepper Sauce

The word 'artichoke' is derived from the Arabic *al-kharshuf*, which became *alcarchofa* in Spanish, then *articiocco* in Italy, and finally 'artichoke' in English. So any idea that the 'choke' refers to difficulties in eating is misplaced, because the English word merely reflects its Arabic origin. Traditionally, artichoke flower heads (the edible parts) appear in Egyptian markets in March and April, so they are snapped up when they are available.

In this recipe the spicy meat filling transforms the artichokes into a rich and satisfying dish, and the red pepper sauce adds an interesting, slightly sweet counterpoint to the creamy leaves and filling. As if that weren't enough to tempt you, artichokes also contain high amounts of luteolin, which means that they help to lower blood cholesterol, so they are good for your health too.

Serves: 4–6

INGREDIENTS
1 tablespoon ghee or butter
1 medium onion, chopped
500 g (1 lb) ground beef
140 g (5 oz) thickened tomato paste
Sea salt and freshly ground black pepper
½ teaspoon ground cinnamon
½ teaspoon ground allspice (optional)
12 large artichokes
Dash of lemon juice

Red pepper sauce
1½ tablespoons vegetable oil
1 small onion or 2 shallots, peeled and chopped
2 red peppers, deseeded and chopped
1 cup (250 ml) tomato sauce or passata
3 tablespoons fresh basil
½ teaspoon salt
Pinch of freshly ground black pepper
½ teaspoon mixed spice
1 large tomato, chopped
2 cups (500 ml) chicken stock or water

- Begin by preparing the meat stuffing. Heat the butter in a large pan, add the onion, and fry over medium heat until golden brown. Add the mince and cook over a high heat for around 15 minutes, until it is browned and almost all the liquid has evaporated. Add the tomato sauce, salt, pepper, spices, and 2 cups (500 ml) water, and bring to the boil. Reduce the heat and simmer uncovered for 30 minutes or until the meat is cooked and the liquid has reduced, but the meat is not completely dry. Set aside.

- While the meat is cooking, prepare the artichokes. Trim the tips of the artichoke leaves, cut off the stalks, and cut out the furry center. Put the artichokes in a bowl of water with a dash of lemon juice to soak for 15 minutes.

- Preheat the oven to 180°C (350°F/Gas mark 4).

- Prepare the red pepper sauce. Heat the oil in a pan and gently cook the onion until soft. Stir in the remaining ingredients and bring to the boil, then reduce the heat and simmer for 15 minutes. Blend to a smooth paste.

- Drain the artichokes. Fill the center of each one with the cooked mince and place onto a baking dish. When all the artichokes are on the baking dish, pour over the red pepper sauce.

- Bake for 45–60 minutes or until the artichokes are cooked through. Gently push a fork into the base of one artichoke to test if it is cooked. Serve with flatbread or rice.

Batatis mahshiya | Mince-stuffed Potatoes

This can easily be adjusted to suit the number of diners, and you can vary the spices and add herbs to the sauce according to your personal preferences. The tomato, onion, and balsamic vinegar are lovely together and really boost the flavor. This dish is delicious with a fresh salad.

Serves: 6

INGREDIENTS
Vegetable oil, for frying
1 small red onion, finely chopped
1 clove garlic, crushed
250 g (½ lb) ground beef
2 large tomatoes, finely chopped
1 tablespoon balsamic vinegar
2 tablespoons fresh thyme
Sea salt and freshly ground black pepper
1 teaspoon mixed spice
3 tablespoons thickened tomato paste
1 kg (2 ¼ lb) potatoes
1 cup (250 ml) beef stock or water

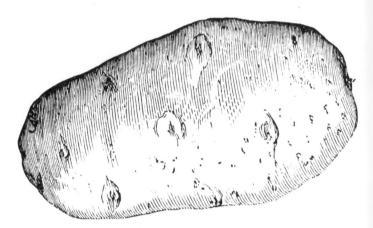

• Preheat the oven to 180°C (350°F/Gas mark 4). Heat some oil in a pan and fry the onion and garlic for several minutes over a medium heat until soft.

• Add the ground beef and continue frying until the meat is browned, breaking up any lumps that form during cooking.

• Add the tomatoes, vinegar, thyme, salt, pepper, mixed spice, and 2 tablespoons of the tomato paste. Fry for a further 2–3 minutes. Remove from the heat.

• Peel and core the potatoes using an apple corer or small knife, making a hole in the center that does not quite reach the bottom end of the potato. Stuff each potato with the meat mixture and press firmly so the mixture is tightly packed.

• Place the stuffed potatoes closely together on a baking dish. Blend together the remaining tomato paste with 1 cup (250 ml) of water or beef stock and bake for 60 minutes, until the liquid has reduced and the potato is cooked through. Serve immediately.

Mesa'aa | Egyptian Moussaka

I used to love eating this dish of layered eggplant and minced meat. It reminds me of summer, when my mother would slice the eggplant and salt it then leave it out in the sun for several hours in a colander to drain out the bitter liquid. She would then fry it in butter and layer it with mince before being baked. I remember going out to check on the eggplant slices when they were salted outside, because I couldn't wait for the *mesa'aa* to be made so I could eat it. This is my comfort food! You can make it using two-thirds beef mince and one-third lamb mince, if you like, which gives the dish a really rich flavor, and subsitute mace or allspice for the mixed spice. We ate this at home with rice and salad.

Serves: 6

INGREDIENTS
1 kg (2¼ lb) eggplant
2 tablespoons salt
Olive oil, for frying and greasing
1 large onion, finely chopped
750 g (1½ lb) beef, minced or ground
400 g (1 can) chopped tomatoes
1 cup (250 ml) tomato sauce or passata
140 g (5 oz) thickened tomato paste
1 teaspoon mixed spice
1 tablespoon thyme, finely chopped
1 tablespoon oregano, finely chopped
1 tablespoon basil, finely chopped
Sea salt and freshly ground black pepper
25 g (1 oz) breadcrumbs

- Cut the eggplant into 1 cm (½ inch) slices. Place the slices in a colander and salt them liberally, tossing to coat them. Cover them with a plate and weigh this down with a can or jar. Place the colander in the sink (or outside as my mum used to do) for at least 30 minutes so that excess moisture and bitterness can be drawn out.

- Remove the excess salt from the eggplant slices by rinsing, then dry them on paper towel and brush them with oil. Fry them in batches over a medium heat for 5 minutes each side until golden. As each batch cooks, remove it to a plate lined with paper towel.

- Heat 1 tablespoon of oil in a large pan over medium heat. Add the onion and fry until translucent. Add the beef and cook for around 15 minutes, until it is browned and almost all the liquid has evaporated. Break up any lumps that form during cooking.

- Add the tomatoes, tomato paste, and tomato sauce or passata, along with the herbs and spices, and cook for 2 minutes.

- Add 2 cups (500 ml) water, bring it to the boil, then reduce the heat and simmer uncovered until the meat is cooked and the liquid has reduced (almost completely evaporated). Season with salt and pepper.

- Heat the oven to 180°C (350°F/Gas mark 4). Grease a 20 by 15 cm (8 by 6 inch) tray with oil and sprinkle the breadcrumbs over. Tap the tray to spread the crumbs in a thin layer and remove any excess.

- Layer half the eggplant over the base, then cover with half the cooked mince. Repeat with another layer of eggplant and the remainder of the meat. Bake, uncovered, for 40–45 minutes or until golden brown on top.

Kusa bi-l-beshamel | Zucchini in Béchamel Sauce

Zucchini with béchamel sauce is a great way to eat any type of zucchini when they are in season and abundant—which in many countries is all summer long. The zucchini is sliced and layered with mince, then topped with béchamel sauce prior to baking. This is another favorite of mine. We ate it with rice and a salad.

Serves: 6

INGREDIENTS

Olive oil, for frying and greasing
1 large onion, finely chopped
2 cloves garlic, crushed
1 kg (2¼ lb) ground beef
280 g (10 oz) thickened tomato paste
1 tablespoon mixed spice
Sea salt and freshly ground black pepper
2¾ cups (690 ml) tomato sauce or passata
1 kg (2¼ lb) zucchini
25 g (1 oz) breadcrumbs

Béchamel sauce
100 g (3½ oz) butter
100 g (3½ oz) plain flour
1½ teaspoon mace or mixed spice
2½ cups (625 ml) full-cream milk
Sea salt and freshly ground black pepper
56 g (2 oz) grated Parmesan cheese

• Heat 1 tablespoon of oil in a large pan over medium heat. Add the onion and garlic and fry until translucent. Add the beef and cook for around 15 minutes, until it is browned and almost all the liquid has evaporated. Break up any lumps that form during cooking.

• Add the tomato paste and mixed spice, and season with salt and pepper.

• Add the tomato sauce or passata and cook for a further 2 minutes before adding 2 cups (500 ml) water. Bring to the boil, then reduce the heat and simmer uncovered until the meat is cooked and the liquid has almost completely evaporated.

• While the meat is cooking, make the béchamel sauce. In a heavy-based saucepan, melt the butter over a medium heat and then stir in the flour. Cook for 2 minutes, add the spices, and cook for a further minute, stirring continuously. Add the milk in small amounts, each time stirring to a smooth paste before adding more. Bring to the boil then reduce the heat and simmer gently for 1–2 minutes. Remove from the heat and stir in the parmesan cheese.

• Heat the oven to 180°C (350°F/Gas mark 4). Cut the zucchini into 1 cm (½ inch) thick slices.

• Grease a 20 by 15 cm (8 by 6 inch) tray with oil and sprinkle the breadcrumbs over. Tap the tray to spread the crumbs in a thin layer and remove any excess. Layer half the zucchini over the base then cover with half the cooked mince. Repeat with another layer of zucchini and the remainder of the meat. Spread the béchamel sauce evenly over the top and bake, uncovered, for 40–45 minutes, or until golden brown.

Gullash bi-l-lahma | Flaky Pastry Bake

Traditionally this dish is made with filo pastry with melted butter brushed between the sheets, but a nice variation on this is to use pre-made puff pastry sheets. The resulting dish is just as tasty but it is quicker to prepare and no butter is required. My mother never made this dish with mushrooms, but I think mince with onions and mushrooms are a perfect match. Cooking the mushrooms in butter gives them a lovely flavor but if you prefer, the mushrooms can be cooked in a little garlic-infused oil or omitted entirely.

Serves: 4

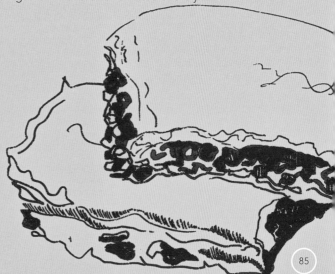

INGREDIENTS
1 tablespoon olive oil
1 large onion, finely chopped
1 clove garlic, crushed
750 g (1½ lb) of minced beef
Salt and pepper to taste
56 g (2 oz) butter
500 g (1 lb) button mushrooms, cleaned and sliced
2 sheets butter puff pastry
2 eggs, lightly beaten
1 cup (250 ml) milk

• Heat the oil in a pan over a medium heat. Add the onion and garlic and fry for 2 minutes.

• Add the minced meat to the pan and fry until browned, breaking up any lumps that form during cooking. Season with salt and pepper. Add ½ cup (125 ml) of water and simmer until the water has evaporated. Set aside to cool.

• In a separate frying pan, melt the butter and sauté the mushrooms on medium heat until soft.

• Heat the oven to 180°C (350°F/Gas mark 4) and lightly grease a baking dish. Place a sheet of ready-rolled puff pastry on the baking dish, spread it with the cooked mince, and then scatter a layer of mushrooms on top. Cover with another sheet of pastry. Cut the pastry bake into squares.

• Beat the eggs and milk together and brush this evenly over the pastry. Bake for 40–45 minutes or until the pastry is golden brown. Serve immediately.

COOK'S TIP

The meat mixture may be prepared and cooked ahead of time and then refrigerated or frozen until required. Thaw out and bring to room temperature before using it for best results. Heat to a temperature of at least 70°C (160°F) for at least 2 minutes before use. The mince should be cooked and cooled. Adding the meat to the pastry while it is still hot will spoil the pastry and result in its uneven cooking.

Arnabit fi-l-forn | Baked Cauliflower

White cauliflower lacks the chlorophyll found in green vegetables like broccoli, cabbage, and kale because the leaves of the plant shield the florets from the sun as they grow (intense sunshine would give the cauliflower heads sunburn). However, around ten years ago a yellow–green cauliflower was developed by crossing a white cauliflower with broccoli, and today you occasionally see purple and orange cauliflowers too. All the different versions are excellent sources of vitamins C and K, and provide lots of fiber.

When selecting cauliflower, look for a clean, compact head (curd) in which the florets have not separated. Check that there are no brown or purple spots as this indicates that the cauliflower is past its nutritional peak. While cauliflower may not be everyone's favorite vegetable, the tomato and cumin in this dish combine nicely to give it an unusual flavor, and may make a few converts.

Serves: 6

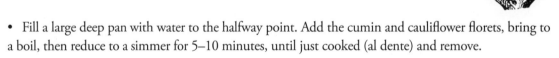

INGREDIENTS
1 tablespoon cumin seeds
1 whole cauliflower, cut into florets
2 onions, peeled
1 kg (2 ¼ lb) gravy beef or chuck casserole steak, cut into 6 pieces
Sea salt and freshly ground black pepper
¼ teaspoon ground nutmeg
28 g (1 oz) ghee or butter
2 tomatoes, thickly sliced
140 g (5 oz) thickened tomato paste

• Fill a large deep pan with water to the halfway point. Add the cumin and cauliflower florets, bring to a boil, then reduce to a simmer for 5–10 minutes, until just cooked (al dente) and remove.

• Cut a cross into the top of one onion, and place it in a pan with the beef, salt, pepper, and nutmeg. Add 4 cups (1 liter) of water, or as much as necessary to cover the meat and onion, and bring to a boil over medium heat. Reduce to a simmer, cover, and leave to cook gently for 20 minutes or so until the beef is cooked. Remove the beef from the pan and reserve the cooking stock.

• While the beef is cooking, preheat the oven to 180°C (350°F/Gas mark 4). Melt the ghee or butter in a pan and fry the cauliflower in batches until lightly golden. Drain each batch on paper towel.

• Slice the remaining onion. Place the sliced onion with the tomato, cauliflower, and beef into a large baking dish. Combine the tomato paste with 1 cup (250 ml) of the reserved beef stock and pour it over the cauliflower. Bake in the oven for 40–45 minutes until the liquid has reduced and the onion is soft. Serve with rice and salad, if desired.

COOK'S TIP
You can use a whole chicken cut into pieces instead of beef chunks for this recipe. Cook using the same method.

Batatis fi-l-forn | Egyptian Roast Beef and Potatoes

This meal is a simple yet hearty dish that is wonderfully warming and filling in winter. My mum served it over rice for a double-carb loading, but added freshness by adding a salad to the table.

Serves: 6

INGREDIENTS
1 kg (2¼ lb) potatoes, peeled and thickly sliced
2 or 3 tomatoes, thickly sliced
1 onion, thickly sliced
1 tablespoon ghee
1 kg (2¼ lb) topside or shin of beef, cut into 10 to 12 pieces
140 g (5 oz) thickened tomato paste
1 teaspoon ground allspice
1 teaspoon salt
½ teaspoon pepper
2 cups (500ml) tomato sauce or passata

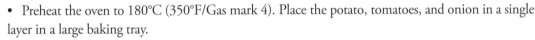

• Preheat the oven to 180°C (350°F/Gas mark 4). Place the potato, tomatoes, and onion in a single layer in a large baking tray.

• Melt the ghee in a pan over a high heat and fry the beef for several minutes until browned.

• Add the tomato paste, spice, and seasoning and fry for around one minute. Then add the tomato sauce or passata and 2½ cups (625 ml) water. Bring to the boil then pour the sauce over the potato, tomatoes, and onion. The meat and potatoes should be at least half covered; if not, add more water.

• Bake in the oven for 2 hours. Check after 1½ hours that there is sufficient liquid—if not, add a little water. Turn the meat if it is browning too much. The dish is cooked when the liquid has reduced, the potato is well cooked, and the meat is tender.

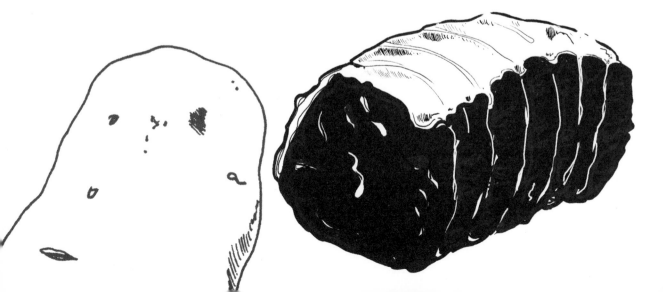

Sanniyit batatis | Mince and Potato Bake

This is the Egyptian take on Shepherd's Pie, but with the mince sandwiched between a mashed potato base and top. It is a simple yet hearty meal that was popular with us as kids—we modernized it by adding a splash of tomato ketchup on top. My mum would sometimes retain some of the beaten egg to spread on top. The version here is a delicious variation by my stepmother, who likes to put breadcrumbs on top, adding texture to the dish by giving it a crunchy surface.

Serves: 6

INGREDIENTS

1 tablespoon butter	*Mashed potato*
1 medium onion chopped	1 kg (2¼ lb) potatoes
450 g (1 lb) ground beef	½ teaspoon sea salt
1½ teaspoons ground allspice	¼ teaspoon freshly ground black pepper
1 teaspoon ground nutmeg	½ teaspoon mixed spice
½ teaspoon ground cinnamon	½ cup (125 ml) milk
½ teaspoon salt	½ cup (125 ml) cream
¼ teaspoon freshly ground black pepper	1 tablespoon butter
25 g (1 oz) dried breadcrumbs	
Olive oil, for drizzling	

• Begin by making the mashed potato. Peel the potatoes and cut them into 2 cm (¾ inch) cubes. Place them in a large pan and add cold water until the potatoes are covered. Bring to the boil, then reduce the heat, and simmer until soft (around 8–10 minutes). Drain and return to the pan. Add the seasoning and spice along with the milk, cream, and butter. Mash until smooth.

• While the potato is cooking, heat the butter in a pan over a medium heat. Add the onion and fry for 2 minutes.

• Add the ground meat to the pan and fry until browned, breaking up any lumps that form during cooking. Add the allspice, nutmeg, and cinnamon, and season with salt and pepper. Cook for 2 minutes until the spices are fragrant, then add ½ cup (125 ml) of water and simmer until the water has evaporated.

• Preheat the oven to 180°C (350°F/Gas mark 4). Grease a 30 by 26 cm (12 by 10 inch) tray and cover with a layer of breadcrumbs, reserving any excess for the top. Place half the potato mixture in a layer over the breadcrumbs, using clean fingertips and dipping them in water as necessary.

• Add the meat, spreading it evenly over the potato. Then use the remaining potato mixture to make a third layer, on top of the meat. Drizzle oil over the potato and sprinkle with the remaining breadcrumbs to coat. Bake for 45 minutes until the top is golden brown. Serve hot with vegetables or a salad.

Macarona forn | Pasta Bake with Béchamel Sauce

I have fond memories of this dish. We often have this now at family gatherings because it is a big hit with the kids and adults alike. It's tasty and filling—it combines pasta with meat and white sauce like a twist on lasagne. I often add finely diced vegetables to the mince while cooking to make a more complete meal, so feel free to improvise here if you want to. Vegetables such as carrot, celery, capsicum, and mushroom all work well and tend to go unnoticed by fussy eaters, so it's a good way of sneaking more vegetables into children's mouths.

Serves: 6–8

INGREDIENTS
1 tablespoon ghee or butter
1 large onion chopped
1 kg (2¼ lb) ground beef
1 teaspoon sea salt
¼ teaspoon freshly ground black pepper
1 teaspoon mace
240 g (8½ oz) thickened tomato paste
2¾ cups (690 ml) tomato sauce or passata
500 g (1 lb) rigatoni or penne pasta
¼ cup breadcrumbs

Béchamel sauce
2 tablespoons butter
¼ cup (30 g) plain flour
Sea salt and pepper
½ teaspoon mace or mixed spice
2½ cups (625 ml) milk
56 g (2 oz) grated tasty cheese
28 g (1 oz) grated parmesan cheese

- Begin by making the meat sauce. Heat the ghee or butter in a pan over a medium heat and fry the onion until soft and golden brown. Add the mince, seasoning, and spices and continue to fry, breaking up any lumps that form. Continue to cook until the meat has browned and all the meat juices have evaporated.

- Add the tomato paste and cook for a further minute before adding the tomato sauce or passata and 2 cups (500 ml) water. Reduce the heat and simmer, stirring occasionally, for 30–45 minutes or until the meat is cooked and there is only a thin film of liquid. Set aside.

- Preheat the oven to 180°C (350°F/Gas mark 4). Fill a large pot with water and bring to the boil. Add the pasta and cook as directed on the packaging. Strain, but do not rinse, as pasta should be sticky for this recipe.

- While the pasta is cooking, make the béchamel sauce. In a saucepan, melt the butter over a medium heat and add the flour. Cook for 2 minutes, stirring continuously, then add the seasoning and spices and cook for a further minute, still stirring. Add a little of the milk and stir to a smooth paste before adding more. Continue to add the milk in small amounts, stirring all the time to prevent any lumps forming. Bring to the boil, then reduce the heat and gently simmer until the sauce has thickened. Remove from the heat. Add the cheese and mix until smooth.

- Grease a large tray—around 30 by 26 cm (12 by 10 inches)—and coat it with breadcrumbs. Reserve any excess. Using half the pasta, add a layer of pasta to the tray so that it covers the base of the tray.

- Add the meat on top of the pasta, spreading it evenly across the tray.

- Layer the remaining pasta evenly over the meat and cover with the béchamel sauce. Sprinkle the remaining breadcrumbs over the top. Bake for 45–50 minutes or until the top is golden brown.

Beid iskutlandi | Scotch Egg

This dish gets its name from the English dish called 'Scotch Egg' which consists of a shelled, hard-boiled egg wrapped in a ground sausage meat mixture coated in breadcrumbs and then deep-fried. Typically, Scotch eggs are eaten cold and served with salad and pickles. This version is probably more like a meatloaf—the eggs are boiled and shelled then wrapped up in a spiced minced meat and baked.

Serves: 4

INGREDIENTS
500 g (1 lb) ground beef
½ teaspoon sea salt
¼ teaspoon freshly ground black pepper
½ teaspoon mixed spice
½ teaspoon ground allspice
1 onion, finely chopped or minced
1 egg, lightly beaten, plus 4 eggs, hard-boiled and shelled

- Preheat the oven to 180°C (350°F/Gas mark 4). In a large bowl, combine the beef, seasoning, spices, onion, and beaten egg and mix well.

- Place a piece of aluminum foil (approximately A4 size, or 8½ x 11 inches) on the table. Spoon all the meat mixture onto it. Flatten out the mixture so it forms a rectangular shape about ¼ inch (0.5 cm) thick.

- Place the boiled eggs in a line along the center, then roll the edges of the meat mixture together using the foil to lift it into position. Once the meat is rolled, fold in the sides to seal in the boiled eggs.

- Place on a baking tray or loaf tin and cook for 30 minutes until the meat has cooked, then open up the foil and leave it for another 15 minutes to brown. Remove from the oven, slice, and serve.

Tagen moza | Lamb Tagine

I love lamb shanks, which form the rich base of this dish. When the meat is well cooked it is so incredibly tender that it falls off the bone. In this recipe the shanks are slow cooked with potatoes and tomato, tucked inside a tagine in the oven. As with most dishes, the flavor of the meat will be enhanced if you use a homemade stock using lamb or beef bones, but you could use a stock cube if pressed for time—you will need 2 cups (500 ml) of lamb or beef stock.

   I generally make the stock the day before I need it, which not only makes it easy to throw this dish together, but also means that you can leave it in the fridge overnight so that the fat will rise to the top and solidify, making it very easy to remove. This makes the dish lighter and healthier than if all the fat was used from the stock.

Serves: 4

INGREDIENTS
4 large potatoes
4 lamb shanks
1 large onion, sliced
1 large tomato, sliced
2 tablespoons thickened tomato paste
Sea salt and freshly ground black pepper

Stock
4 lamb bones
Sea salt and freshly ground black pepper
2 bay leaves
1 large onion, peeled with a cross cut into the top

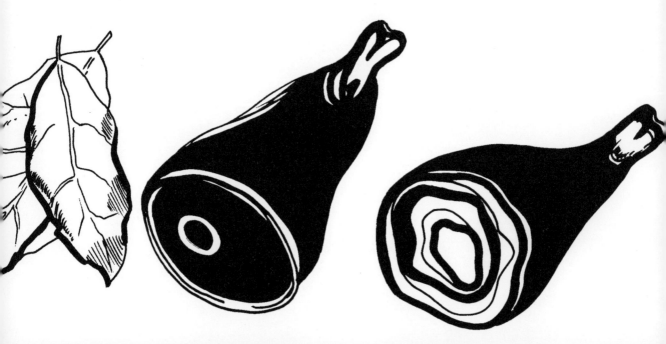

- Begin by making the stock. Place all the ingredients in a large pan or stock pot. Add just enough water to cover the bones and bring it to the boil over a high heat. Remove any impurities that rise to the surface, then reduce the heat and leave to simmer uncovered for 45–60 minutes. Add more water if the liquid reduces too much during the cooking time.

- After an hour, taste the stock to check the seasoning, remove the bones and then place back onto the heat to reduce further—aim for about 2 cups (500 ml) of liquid. Remove any fat from the surface and reserve the stock.

- Preheat the oven to 180°C (350°F/Gas mark 4). Peel and thickly slice the potatoes.

- Place the lamb shanks and vegetables in a large tagine or roasting dish so that they are well distributed.

- Place the tomato paste in a jug and add a little stock. Stir to dissolve the paste, then add more stock to make it up to 2 cups (500 ml). Season with salt and pepper if required, then pour the liquid over the shanks and vegetables. Pour over ½ cup (125 ml) of water and place the tagine or roasting dish in the oven.

- If using a tagine, cover with the lid and bake for 2 hours; if using a roasting dish, leave it uncovered and bake for 60 minutes or until the meat is coming away from the bone and the potato is cooked. After an hour of cooking, I usually remove some of the liquid (to use in soup) and take off the tagine lid, then allow the dish to cook for a further 30 minutes so that the meat develops a lovely color before serving.

Bamya |
Okra, Lamb, and Tomato Stew

Okra, which is also known as 'ladies' fingers,' is a small member of the mallow family, which also includes hollyhocks and hibiscus. The edible part is a thin, green vegetable pod containing small white seeds arranged in vertical rows. It is rich in nutrients, high in antioxidants, very low in calories, and some studies have found that it even helps to lower cholesterol levels. This powerhouse of a vegetable has a surprisingly mild flavor but an unusual texture, which comes from it being rather mucilaginous—this makes it very sticky when cut, and works as a natural thickener during cooking. While okra can be cut and used in soups and stews, this dish is typically made with whole okra pods. If you're unable to buy fresh okra, you can often find it in frozen form in Mediterranean grocery stores.

Serves: 4

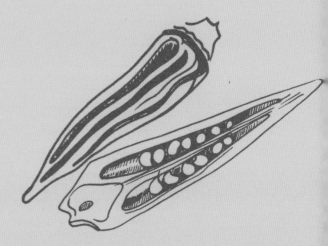

INGREDIENTS
2 tablespoons oil
1 onion, finely chopped
1–2 cloves garlic
500 g (1 lb) lamb tenderloin or shortloin
1 teaspoon salt
¼ teaspoon ground pepper
½ teaspoon mixed spice
140 g (5 oz) thickened tomato paste
2 cups (500 ml) tomato sauce or passata
500 g (1 lb) young okra, frozen or fresh
1 tablespoon lemon juice

• Heat the oil in a large heavy-based saucepan over a medium heat, then fry the onion and garlic for 2 minutes until lightly golden.

• Add the meat and cook it until it is lightly browned and most of the liquid has evaporated. Add the salt, pepper, spice, tomato paste, and sauce, and cook for a further 2 minutes.

• Ensure there is enough liquid to cover the meat, adding a little water if necessary. Bring to the boil over a high heat then reduce the heat and simmer gently, covered, for 45–60 minutes, or until the meat is cooked and very tender.

• While the meat is cooking, make sure the okra is free from bruising and cut off any stalk tops. Once the meat is cooked, add the okra and cook for a further 15 minutes. Add the lemon juice and stir to combine. Serve with rice.

بامية

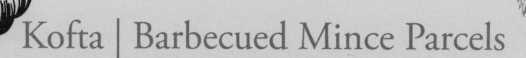

Kofta | Barbecued Mince Parcels

These meat parcels are similar to skinless sausages, but they are packed with flavor. Made of ground meat (usually beef or lamb) mixed with onion, herbs, and spices, they are grilled or barbequed for a crispy finish. My mother and Aunty Nadia made *kofta* this way, simply combining the meat with onions and parsley before shaping and cooking. We often had *kofta* in summer; it was cooked on the barbecue and wrapped in lacy, fatty netting to keep the meat from drying out and burning. I now know that the 'netting' is a form of meat cut known as the 'greater omentum'—a fatty membrane that descends from the stomach and lies over an animal's internal organs. It is often called 'caul fat' and in Arabic it is known as *mandeel*. While it is not commonly used, it can be bought from selected butchers but may need to be ordered, so ask ahead of time. I have found at least three days' notice is best if this is not something that your butcher usually stocks. If you can track this down it is well worth the trouble—it is easy to use and stops the problem of burning the *kofta* outside while leaving it raw in the center. Otherwise cook the *kofta* over coals instead of direct heat. Using a beef and lamb mix also helps with cooking over a barbecue as it means the *kofta* has a high fat content and the fat will render, helping the cooking process as well as giving flavor to the meat.

Serves: 4–6

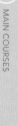

INGREDIENTS
500 g (1 lb) ground beef
500 g (1 lb) ground lamb
2 onions, finely minced
½ tablespoon salt
¼ tablespoon ground pepper
2 cloves garlic, crushed
1 teaspoon allspice
½ teaspoon mixed spice
1 bunch flat-leaf parsley, finely chopped
2 sheets caul fat (optional)

VARIATION
The meat mixture may be used to make kebabs: simply form the mixture into sausages and then wrap them around a skewer before cooking. If using wooden skewers, soak them in water for 15 minutes beforehand to stop them burning while cooking.

• Combine all ingredients except for the caul fat in a large bowl and use your hands to mix them together really well. Light the barbecue.

• If using caul fat, stretch out the fat net on a board or clean surface. The fat often comes with sections of varying thicknesses and it is easiest to use the thinnest parts, so cut out any very thick sections of fat. Pat some meat into the shapes of little sausages and place them at the edge of the caul fat, then roll the fat to cover the meat, making sure it overlaps a little. Cut it away from the caul fat sheet and repeat, making little sausages until the caul fat is used up.

• When the barbecue is ready, place the kofta on it, cut side of fat down, and use a gentle heat until cooked through. A charcoal or wood barbecue imparts a lovely smoky flavor to the kofta. Serve when cooked through.

Kofta ma'liya | Fried Turkey and Apple Kofta

My Aunty Evon inspired this method of making *kofta*, but since there is an abundance of beef in Egyptian cooking I like to use turkey mince here for a change. The apple is great with the mince because it adds tartness and lends some moisture to the *kofta*. This *kofta* is also coated in breadcrumbs, which gives it a crunchy coating and makes it a lovely twist on traditional *kofta*.

Serves: 4

INGREDIENTS
500 g (1 lb) turkey mince
1 Granny Smith apple, peeled and grated
1 small onion, finely chopped or grated
2 tablespoons fresh thyme
Sea salt and freshly ground black pepper
1 egg, beaten
Breadcrumbs, for coating
Oil, for frying

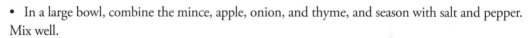

• In a large bowl, combine the mince, apple, onion, and thyme, and season with salt and pepper. Mix well.

• Shape the meat mixture into long flat strips. Put the egg in a bowl and the breadcrumbs onto a plate. For each strip, dip it first into the egg and then lightly press each side into the breadcrumbs so the meat is completely covered.

• Heat the oil in a frying pan over medium heat. Add a few strips at a time to the pan, cooking each batch for 3 minutes on each side or until the breadcrumbs are golden brown and the meat is cooked through. Serve with tomato chutney or tomato ketchup.

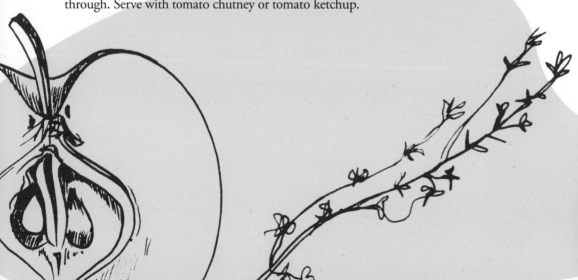

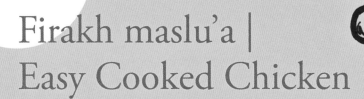

Firakh maslu'a |
Easy Cooked Chicken

My memories of this chicken dish go hand in hand with *molokhiya* (page 120), and I have found that cooking chicken this way is great for kids because it is so much healthier than fried chicken takeouts. It is also a great way to introduce little ones to meat when they have moved beyond the puréed vegetable stage—drumsticks are very easy for little fingers to hold (but always supervise kids while they are eating anything with bones). I often use Maryland pieces (the thigh and drumstick together), which are slightly fatty but more tender than chicken breast pieces. I remove any excess fat from the chicken but leave the skin on for cooking, as the skin is easily removed after cooking if you prefer skinless chicken. The leftovers from this dish are great in pasta sauce—simply remove the chicken from the bone, roughly chop it, and add to pasta sauce with frozen vegetables for a super-easy pasta meal.

Serves: 4

INGREDIENTS
4 chicken Maryland joints (thigh and drumstick together)
1 onion, peeled and with a cross cut into the top
3 dried bay leaves
Sea salt and freshly ground black pepper

• Remove any excess fat from the chicken pieces and place them into a large pan. Cover with water, add the onion, bay leaf, and salt and pepper, and place over a medium heat.

• Bring to a boil, removing any foam or impurities that rise to the surface. Turn the heat down to a simmer, and cook for around 20 minutes, continuing to skim any impurities off the surface as they arise. Check that the chicken is cooked through: the meat should easily be pulled away from the bone and any juices should be clear.

• Drain the chicken, reserving the stock for use in other recipes. Serve alongside *molokhiya* (page 120) or *fatta* (page 118).

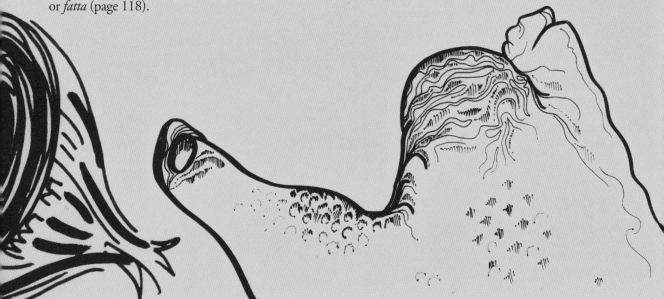

Firakh bi-l-tom wi-l-limun | Roast Chicken with Garlic and Lemon

Roast chicken is definitely a favorite meal of mine. Cooked correctly it is so juicy and tasty, and this marinade is very easy and tastes great. I love the combined flavors of the of rice, chicken, and feta cheese and I always associate them together. This quantity is for four Maryland pieces of chicken for four people but as with most recipes, use any pieces you like and adjust for the number of people.

Serves: 4

INGREDIENTS
4 chicken Maryland joints (thigh and drumstick together)

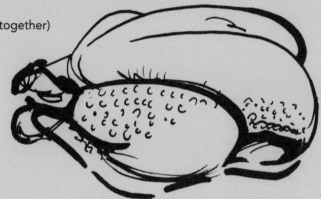

Marinade
1 onion, minced
1 tomato, very finely diced
Juice of ½ lemon
1 teaspoon sea salt flakes
½ teaspoon freshly ground black pepper
½ teaspoon nutmeg or mixed spice

• Preheat the oven to 180°C (350°F/Gas mark 4). Combine all the marinade ingredients in a bowl and mix well.

• Taking each chicken piece in turn, separate the skin from the flesh over the drumstick and thigh and rub the marinade under and over the skin.

• Place the chicken pieces in a baking dish and cover with any remaining marinade. Roast in the oven for 45 to 60 minutes until cooked. The skin should be crisp and the juices should run clear when the chicken is tested with a skewer at its thickest point. Serve with rice and salad, and perhaps some pickles and feta cheese.

VARIATION

Another way I like this is to substitute lamb chops for the chicken. Using 4 lamb chops, make a marinade by blending 2 onions, 2 peeled tomatoes, 1 clove garlic, 1 tablespoon mixed spice, and some salt and pepper in a food processor. Add a little water if necessary to help it form a paste-like consistency. Place the lamb chops in a large pan, add the marinade and ½ cup (125 ml) water. Cover and simmer for 2 hours on low heat until tender. Serve over rice.

Firakh mahshiya fireek | Fireek-stuffed Chicken

Fireek (also known as freekeh and farika) is a grain harvested from green, immature durum wheat. It can be found in delicatessens, Middle-Eastern grocery shops, and some supermarkets, and it makes a great stuffing for chicken and pigeon (page 107). If you can't find fireek, you could substitute it with bulgur wheat. When I have time, I love to use this stuffing for roast chicken—the grains are perfectly softened by chicken fat and perfumed oh-so-subtly by onion. Seriously, it is delicious, and I eagerly look forward to the meal after the aroma fills the kitchen during cooking.

Serves: 4–6

INGREDIENTS
1 tablespoon butter
1 small onion, finely chopped
110 g (4 oz) fireek
½ cup jasmine or long-grain rice
½ teaspoon sea salt flakes
¼ teaspoon freshly ground black pepper
1 whole, large chicken

• Preheat the oven to 180°C (350°F/Gas mark 4). Melt the butter in a saucepan and fry the onion over a medium heat until lightly browned.

• Lower the heat, add the fireek and rice, and cook, stirring gently, for around 5 minutes (until the color changes slightly). Season with salt and pepper.

• Take the whole chicken and stuff the rice and fireek mixture into the breast cavity. Close the cavity by lacing 2 or 3 skewers over it or by sewing it shut with a heavy thread.

• Place the chicken breast-side-up on a greased rack inside a deep roasting dish. Cook on the center shelf of the oven for 25 minutes per 500 g (1 lb) plus 20 minutes. Check that it is cooked by pulling a leg away from the body and piercing between the leg and body—the juices should run clear and have no pink tinge. Stand for about 10 minutes before serving.

COOK'S TIP
Depending on the size of the chicken, you may have some stuffing left over. If so, push your fingers under the breast skin to make a pocket and then place any remaining stuffing under the skin. When cooking, you can keep the chicken especially moist by using an oven-safe roasting bag; just pierce the bag 4 or 5 times with a skewer to vent.

Hamam | Tender Poached Squab

Pigeon is commonly farmed and eaten in Egypt, and the birds live in quite distinctive mud-brick houses—these tall, finger-like domes are covered with entry holes for the birds in a myriad of decorative patterns. Pigeon meat is darker than chicken and its taste is closer to duck. Commercially raised or farmed birds (squab) take less time to cook than traditionally raised birds, and they are suitable for roasting, grilling, or searing. The meat from older or wild pigeons is tougher and better suited to casseroles and slow-cooked stews. Since these birds are relatively expensive to buy, this is not an everyday kind of dish, but it makes a delicious treat. Fireek is the only ingredient that may be tricky to source; if you can't find it, you could use bulgur wheat and the end result would also be delicious.

Serves: 1–2

INGREDIENTS
1½ onions, peeled
1½ tablespoons ghee or butter
55 g (2 oz) fireek
100 g (3½ oz) white rice
2 pigeons
1 bay leaf
Sea salt
Freshly ground black pepper
Fried quail eggs, to serve (optional)

• Finely chop ½ onion. Melt half the butter or ghee in a saucepan and fry the onion for 2 or 3 minutes over a medium heat.

• Add the fireek and rice along with ¾ cup (180 ml) water. Cook for 15 minutes or until the water has been absorbed (note that the grains will not yet be fully cooked).

• Divide the stuffing between the two pigeons, filling the breast cavity of each one. Close the breast cavity by sewing with heavy thread or by lacing with 2 or 3 skewers.

• Take a pan big enough to fit both birds and fill it with water to around the halfway point. Cut a cross into the top of the remaining onion and add it to the pan along with the bay leaf, salt, and pepper.

• Put the birds into the pan and reduce the heat to low. Make sure the birds are covered with water—add more if required. Simmer for around 15 minutes then check to see if cooked: insert a skewer into a thick part of the bird and check that the juices are running clear.

• When the birds are cooked, heat the remaining ghee or butter in a frying pan and fry the birds over a medium heat, turning frequently, until they are a lovely golden brown color. Serve with fried quail eggs, if desired.

Arnab | Twice-cooked Rabbit

We ate rabbit very occasionally at home, but it can be a nice change from the usual beef and chicken. The cooking time depends on the age of the rabbit—older rabbits are tougher and need longer cooking—and the rabbit is cooked twice to remove any impurities in the meat. Wild rabbit has a more game-like, tougher meat than the farmed animals, and it's probably best to avoid it: wild rabbits may be carrying the disease Myxomatosis, which is not known to affect humans, but I think it's best to remain cautious.

Serves: 4

INGREDIENTS
1 rabbit
Salt for cleansing meat and seasoning
2 bay leaves
1 large onion, halved
Freshly ground black pepper
28 g (1 oz) ghee or butter

- To prepare the rabbit, wash the meat well and remove any internal organs if still present. Rub the meat well with salt and then rinse, to cleanse and prepare the flesh.

- Cut the rabbit into 6 pieces (or leave whole, if you prefer) and put it into a large stock pot. Cover with water and bring to the boil over a high heat. Reduce the heat, simmer for 30 minutes, then drain and discard the cooking liquid.

- Place the rabbit back into the stock pot and cover it with fresh water. Add the bay leaves, onion, and seasoning. Cover, bring to the boil, then reduce heat to low, simmering for 30–40 minutes until the meat is tender.

- Remove the rabbit and reduce the stock if you want to reserve it for future use: simply boil the liquid uncovered for 20–30 minutes.

- In a large frying pan, melt the ghee or butter. Add the whole or pieces of rabbit and fry the meat until golden. Serve.

Kibda ma'liya bi-l-tom | Garlic-fried Chicken Liver

Chicken livers are probably mostly associated with paté, which is something I first tasted as an adult, but I do recall my mother saying that we used to love chicken livers as kids (I think we stopped eating them when we got old enough to know what they were). My dad tells me that his mum used to cook livers and put them in sandwiches, but we didn't have them like that at home. Livers can easily be overcooked and become tough, but if they are cooked well they have a soft, delicate texture and flavor. Nutritionally, chicken livers are something of a powerhouse: they contain all nine of the essential amino acids, are very rich in iron, and are a great source of protein. This recipe is how we had livers at home.

Serves: 2–4

INGREDIENTS
250 g (8 oz) chicken liver
1 tablespoon ghee or butter
1 or 2 cloves garlic, crushed
Juice of ½ lemon
Sea salt and freshly ground black pepper

- Check the chicken livers for any dark patches. Trim where necessary, then cut the livers into slices.
- Melt the ghee or butter in a frying pan and add the garlic. Fry for 1 minute before adding the liver.
- When the liver has cooked through, remove it from the heat. Drizzle with lemon juice and season lightly. Serve over rice or with warm, fresh flatbread, or as a side to *koshari* (page 50).

Mukh maʿ el-beid | Lamb Brains with Egg

I do not regularly make meals with lamb brains at home, but I do remember my parents serving them to me when I was young. My mum would cook them like a schnitzel: dipped in flour, then beaten egg, then breadcrumbs, and fried. My dad, on the other hand, grew up eating lamb brains cooked with egg, and I'm including his recipe here.

Serves: 2

INGREDIENTS
2 lamb brains
1 teaspoon salt
1 tablespoon lemon juice
1 tablespoon ghee or butter
2 eggs
Sea salt and freshly ground black pepper

• Poach the lamb brains by placing them in a large pan and covering them with water; add salt and lemon juice. Bring to the boil briefly then reduce the heat, allowing them to simmer for approximately 5 minutes.

• Drain the brains, place them on a chopping board, and dice them.

• In a frying pan, melt the butter or ghee over a medium heat. Add the diced brain and fry until golden brown.

• Crack open the eggs over the pan, so that they fall on top of the brains. Stir once or twice until the egg is cooked. Season with salt and pepper. Serve with rice or warm flatbread.

Mukh bi-l-bu'sumat| Golden Crumbed Parcels

Crunchy, golden, fried food seems to have a natural appeal, and these crunchy parcels have proved popular among those adventurous enough to try them. My dad grew up eating lamb brains with egg (page 111), but my mum preferred this recipe and used to make these for us when I was growing up.

Serves: 2

INGREDIENTS
2 lamb brains
30 g (1 oz) plain flour
Pinch of salt and pepper
1 egg, beaten
40 g (1½ oz) dried breadcrumbs
2 tablespoons vegetable oil, for frying

• Gently pat dry the lamb brains using a paper towel. Put the flour in a bowl with a pinch of salt and pepper and mix together. Place a bowl containing the beaten egg close to the flour bowl, and a third containing breadcrumbs next to that. Dip the brains into the flour to coat them, then dip them into the egg, and finally, roll them in the breadcrumbs to coat well. Dip them a second time in the egg and breadcrumbs, pressing down gently to get a thick coat. Refrigerate for 10 minutes.
• Heat the oil in a small frying pan and then fry the brains for a few minutes turning until golden brown.

Samak ma'li | Fried Whole Fish

We didn't eat a great deal of seafood at home, so I didn't really experience the wide variety available until I was older. When we did have fish it was usually a whole, white-fleshed variety that was either fried in oil or baked—it was always seasoned basically the same for either method of cooking. I remember sitting at the table combing through a whole fish on my plate, being careful to find all the bones and remove them. I'm sure there was more than one occasion when I missed a bone and had it stick somewhere in my throat! Generally, though, I used to love having fish at home when my mum made it and I would always check whether she was making red rice. Red rice is short grain rice that has been cooked with tomato paste—it was reserved just for serving with fish. This recipe was often served at home with tahini (page 36) and salmon-colored rice (page 24).

It is always best to buy fresh fish wherever possible, and any firm, white-fleshed fish works well here. Ask your fishmonger or your server at the supermarket fish counter to scale and gut the fish; or save time and reduce the potential hazard of choking on bones by using fillets.

Serves: 4

INGREDIENTS
4 firm white-fleshed fish fillets, such as Nile perch
Plain flour, for dipping
Vegetable or olive oil, for frying

Fish Marinade
2 cloves garlic, crushed
1 teaspoon ground cumin
Juice of 1 lemon
Sea salt and freshly ground black pepper

• Make a marinade of garlic, cumin, lemon, and salt and pepper.

• Wash the fish, dry it with paper towel, then rub the marinade in and around the whole fish so it is well-coated. Place the fish in a bowl in the refrigerator for 1–2 hours.

• Put a little plain flour on a board and dip the fish into it, coating all sides before shaking off any excess. Place a frying pan over medium-high heat, add the oil, and add the fish once the oil is hot. Fry for 3–4 minutes on each side. Remove, drain on paper towel, and serve immediately.

COOK'S TIP
You can use the same marinade to cook a fish on the grill or barbecue. Just omit the flour and drizzle the fish with a little oil before cooking.

Samak fi-l-forn bi-l-fireek | Baked Fish with Fireek

Shopping for and cooking whole fish may be a little intimidating but it is actually quite easy. Firstly, to select fresh fish, look at the eyes to see how clear and plump they are (fish that are no longer very fresh have cloudy eyes that dry and eventually collapse). Secondly, check the gills: They should look wet and a lively red/orange/brown color, not dried or dark brown. The smell of fish is important too. A whole fish will smell like a fish, of course, but it should smell like a fish that's been recently plucked from marine or fresh waters. If it's starting to smell unpleasant, steer clear. Lastly, a gentle press of the fish's flesh will see it spring back if it is fresh. If a dent remains in the flesh or it doesn't recover at all, it is past its prime.

   Cooking it is just as easy. Ask your fishmonger to scale and gut the fish for you. When you get home, give the fish a soak in salt water, then pat it dry and season it inside and out with a little salt and pepper.

Serves: 4

INGREDIENTS
1 large whole firm white-flesh fish, such as trout, bream, or snapper
1 portion fish marinade (page 114)
225 g (8 oz) fireek
2 tablespoons thickened tomato paste
1 teaspoon ground cumin
Sea salt and freshly ground black pepper
Flour, for coating
Vegetable oil, for frying
1 tablespoon olive oil

• Preheat the oven to 180°C (350°F/Gas mark 4). Prepare and marinate the fish as for fried fish (page 114).

• Wash and drain the fireek, and place it in a large baking dish.

• Combine the tomato paste with 1 cup (250 ml) water. Add the ground cumin and season with salt and pepper. Pour the mixture over the fireek.

• Put a little plain flour on a board and dip the fish into it, coating all sides before shaking off any excess. Place a frying pan over medium-high heat, add the oil, and add the fish once the oil is hot. Fry for 3–4 minutes on each side.

• Put the fried fish on top of the fireek, drizzle olive oil on top, and put the dish in the oven for 15–20 minutes until cooked and fluffy. Serve hot.

Fatta | Stock-soaked Bread with Rice

This is a hearty, carbohydrate-loaded dish that is made by combining rice and dried bread with a chicken stock. It is lovely in winter and very easy to prepare. The word *fatta* means 'soaked bread,' so the key to this dish is the stock—it needs to be good, because the more concentrated the stock, the better the dish. I like to use a double-cooked stock, which I make by reserving the stock from one batch of chicken and reusing it to cook a second batch. The resulting flavor is divine. The chicken that is used to make the stock is served alongside this dish.

Serves: 4–6

INGREDIENTS
1½–2 cups (375–500 ml) double chicken stock (page 21)
2 loaves Lebanese bread
28 g (1 oz) ghee or butter
4 cloves garlic, crushed
3 tablespoons white vinegar
1 serving of rice with vermicelli (page 22)
2 shallots, finely chopped, optional garnish

• Using the boiled chicken reserved from making the stock, remove the chicken meat from the bones and roughly chop.

• Preheat the oven to 200°C (400°F/Gas mark 6). Split the bread into halves and place it in the oven for 10–15 minutes until completely dry and golden brown.

• Break the bread into small pieces over a large bowl or stock pot.

• Heat the stock in a pan; bring it briefly to the boil then turn down the heat so that it is simmering gently.

• In a small pan, melt the butter or ghee and fry the garlic until it is just beginning to change color, then add the vinegar and mix well. Take off the heat and add to the stock.

• Pour the garlic and stock mix over the dried broken bread, stir, then add the rice and combine. Place the buttery mixture in a serving plate and scatter the chopped chicken over the top. Garnish with the finely chopped fresh shallots just before serving.

> **COOK'S TIP**
> Fried shallots can be used instead of fresh ones for the garnish. They can often be found in supermarkets now, as well as Asian grocery stores, or you can simply fry 1–2 fresh, finely chopped shallots in hot oil until golden brown and crisp. Remove, drain on paper towel, and sprinkle over the cooked chicken.

Molokhiya | Mallow Soup

There are not a great number of soup dishes in the Egyptian culinary repertoire that I know of, but there is one undeniably classic dish: *molokhiya*. It is one of Egypt's national dishes and it is believed to have originated during the time of the pharaohs, because it is depicted in pharaonic tomb paintings. During the reign of the Fatimid caliph al-Hakim, over a thousand years ago, the public was banned from eating *molokhiya* and this may explain why it is said that the original name for *molokhiya* is *molokiya*, meaning 'of the kings.'

The soup is famously mucilaginous (moist and sticky) and it is made from the leaves of a herb that is also known as *molokhiya*. My father grew this herb every summer, and still does, only now he picks the leaves with the grandkids and divides them among each of the families so that we can all have a taste of his crop each season. It only grows in the summer, but it can be dried or frozen and eaten all year round. We used to preserve the leaves by picking them, rinsing them several times with water, then spreading them out on sheets of newspaper to dry, tossing them occasionally. Then we would take the dry leaves and chop them as finely as possible, wrap them in plastic, and freeze them for later. Sometimes *molokhiya* is preserved as a powder, by crushing the dried leaves.

To prepare any form of dried *molokhiya*, simply moisten the leaves with a few spoonfuls of water then proceed with the recipe. The chicken can be replaced by 1 rabbit or 500 g (1 lb) topside beef, cut into several large portions. Traditionally, the meat used to make the stock is served on the side, either plainly boiled or fried in ghee until golden brown.

Serves: 4

INGREDIENTS
3 tablespoons ghee
6 cloves garlic, crushed
1½ tablespoons ground coriander
4 cups (1 liter) chicken stock
400 g (14 oz) frozen *molokhiya* leaves or 750 g (27 oz) fresh *molokhiya*, chopped

• Melt the ghee in a frying pan over a medium heat and add the garlic. Cook until lightly browned, then add the coriander. Stir and remove from the heat.

• Place the stock in a pan and bring to the boil, then reduce the heat and add the chopped molokhiya. (If using frozen *molokhiya*, add it to the stock while still frozen.) Leave the pan uncovered and do not stir—just allow the liquid to heat gently until it reaches boiling point, then remove from the heat. Be careful not to overcook *molokhiya* as this can result in separation and a two-layered soup.

• Add the garlic mix to the *molokhiya* and stir to combine. If necessary, add some water to achieve the desired consistency and adjust seasoning to taste.

• Serve immediately in bowls with rice or fresh Lebanese or pita bread. The bread can be broken into pieces and then used to scoop the *molokhiya*, or it can be added to the bowl of soup and eaten with a spoon.

ملوخية

Ul'as | Taro with Swiss Chard

Taro, or colcasia, is known as *ul'as* in Egypt. It is a somewhat ugly-looking root that exudes a sticky sap when cut, but when cooked correctly it makes a delicious and unique-tasting meal. The corms of the Egyptian *ul'as* are larger than those found in North American and European supermarkets.

The hairy skin of the tuber is always peeled before cooking. There are two popular ways to cook it: one is to cut it into slices and cook it with minced meat and tomato sauce; another is to cut it into small cubes and cook it in broth with fresh coriander and Swiss chard, as described below. Kale could be used in place of chard for an equally delicious result. When you are making the chicken stock, reserve the chicken meat to accompany this dish.

Serves: 6

INGREDIENTS
4 cups (1 liter) chicken stock (page 20)
1 kg (2¼ lb) taro
Juice of ½ lemon
170 g (6 oz) Swiss chard
½ bunch cilantro
½ teaspoon sea salt
¼ teaspoon freshly ground black pepper
28 g (1 oz) ghee or butter
7 cloves garlic, crushed

- Heat the stock in a deep pan, bringing it briefly to the boil then turning it down to a gentle simmer. While it is heating, peel the taro and cut it into cubes.

- Add the taro and lemon juice to the pan and leave to simmer for about 25 minutes or until tender.

- Prepare the chard by removing the stems and roughly chopping the leaves. Place it in a large frying pan, along with the cilantro, ½ cup (125 ml) water, and salt and pepper. Stir over high heat until the chard has wilted. Transfer to a blender and blend to a purée.

- Melt the ghee or butter in a frying pan or skillet, add the garlic, and fry until it begins to brown. Add the puréed chard and cook for a further 5 minutes.

- Add the chard mixture to the taro and bring to the boil. Serve hot with rice and boiled chicken.

'Ads | Silky Lentil Soup

This is one of the few soups traditionally eaten during the cooler months in Egypt. It is warm and nutritious, and the flavors of cumin and lemon are wonderful with the lentils. It's easy to find the ingredients in supermarkets and lentils are one of the least expensive sources of protein. They are also a good source of dietary fiber and carbohydrates.

My mum's way of making this involved using a special strainer, which pushed the soup through holes and she turned the handle. I don't have one of these, so I did try pushing the soup through a strainer using a spoon, but soon realized that this took huge effort and was very messy. My (much easier) way is to blend the soup using a stick blender, which produces a wonderfully smooth soup. It achieves the same result as my mum's strainer but with half the fuss.

I taught this recipe to a group of participants in one of my Egyptian cooking classes, and of all the classes and recipes this one stands out to me—mainly because it came with such a flood of compliments. With such easily accessible ingredients, this recipe is basic in nature but really full of flavor. It's so warm and comforting on a cold winter's day.

Serves: 6

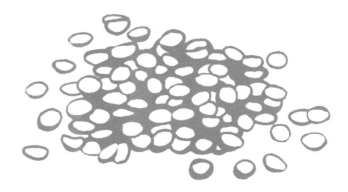

INGREDIENTS
1 tablespoon ghee or butter
1 medium onion, chopped
300 g (10½ oz) red lentils
2 teaspoons ground cumin
2 tablespoons lemon juice
½ teaspoon sea salt

- Melt the ghee or butter in a deep pan over medium heat and add the chopped onion. Fry for 5 minutes or until lightly browned.

- Meanwhile, wash and strain the lentils. When the onion is cooked, remove it to a plate and add the lentils to the pot along with 4 cups (1 liter) of water, adding more water if the soup is too thick. Bring this to the boil then reduce the heat, cover, and leave to simmer for 30 minutes until cooked.

- Carefully use a stick blender to blend the soup until smooth. Add the cumin and lemon juice and blend again. Check for seasoning before adding salt. Serve with the fried onion on top.

COOK'S TIP
You can use chicken stock here rather than water, for a richer taste. Simply add water to the stock if necessary. This can also be served in a more liquid form as a soup, with fresh Lebanese bread on the side or with small pieces of dried bread broken into the soup. To do this, split the bread into halves, place in a fairly hot oven (200°C/400 °F/Gas mark 6) for 10–15 minutes then break into pieces before sprinkling them over the soup.

بقلاوة

SWEETS

دهربس

SWEETS

The Arabic word *halawiyat* is used for all sweet things, including cakes, cookies, and desserts. Many Egyptian households have some sort of sweet prepared and ready for unexpected but warmly welcomed guests, along with tea *(shay)* or coffee *(ahwa)*. It is almost rude not to offer a sweet or cookies with a drink and just as rude not to accept, which may be why I have developed such a sweet tooth. I often enjoyed an after-school snack of sweet couscous *(kuskusi, page 160)*, which I could make myself, or would ask mum to make almond rice pudding *(roz bi-l-laban, page 144)* or noodles with milk *(sha'riya bi-l-laban, page 145)*.

Christmas was (and still is) a favorite time of year for me because throughout that period cookies would flow like a river out of the kitchen, and the scent of sugar and butter filled the house. The just-baked cookies were divided into containers and would then wait patiently to be given to family and friends when they visited. I have always loved this idea and try to continue the tradition, even though it is somewhat challenging with three young children to entertain.

This chapter is a collection of the sweet things that we ate at home. As with almost every dish, the ingredients or proportions can be altered somewhat—so if your preference is for a more milky rice pudding, feel free to add more milk. You can vary the syrup flavor from vanilla to orange blossom or rose water. Where a recipe calls for nuts, you can use whichever ones you like best or those that are in season and easily available. When I asked my mother whether it was all right to substitute one type of nut for another, she simply said, "Why not? It's not going to say no."

You are sure to find something delicious among these recipes that will work for every occasion, from children's treats to work functions and family celebrations. My mum used to prepare sweets for local church functions and parties, and I have often felt that I'm following in her footsteps as I prepared a tray of *basbousa* (pages 132–37) or a batch of *kahk* (page 164) for my work colleagues. It seems that no matter what the occasion or what sweet dish I took with me, I always came home with an empty container and lots of requests for recipes and more food at future functions. Welcome to the sweet world of Egyptian cooking.

Mrabba | Homemade Jam

I know that there is an art to preserving food and making jam, but I keep recalling how easy it looked when my mum did it. We had a backyard that my dad nurtured and which gave us an ample supply of plums, apricots, lemons, almonds, walnuts, pomegranate, figs, and grape leaves (grapes not so much). He grew strawberries too and we routinely had strawberry jam. Mum also made jam out of the plums, apricots, and figs when the supply was there. In our house there was a dedicated cupboard in the kitchen just for housing all the jars of jam. I don't recall a time when the jam cupboard was empty or that we ever had store-bought jam.

My absolute favorite is fig jam—if you are a fan of figs, as I am, this one is for you. Beautifully sweet, it is not dissimilar to popping candy in texture because of the tiny exploding seeds from the figs. I would never dream of trying to remove the seeds for that reason, and the same goes for strawberries and raspberries. However, if you want a smoother jam you could put it through a strainer before bottling.

I am slowly working on cultivating an edible garden and would love to have a garden as productive as my dad's. But until then I make do by searching around the markets and shops for the ripest fruit in season. When selecting fruit for making jam, remember that you will need some fruit that is not fully ripe, as this will contain a greater level of pectin than the very ripe fruit. Pectin is what makes jam set. Fruit that is still slightly green at the top is ideal: Don't cut the green part off—just wash the fruit, peel or remove the stones from plums and apricots, then cut into small pieces and weigh along with the riper fruit.

Use a pan that is wider than it is deep, because this will allow the fruit to boil faster, and choose a non-aluminum pan, because aluminum can affect the jam's color and flavor. Glass jars are ideal for storing the jam, but they must be sterile or bacteria will make the jam inedible. My mum used to sterilize jars over an open flame, but you can more safely sterilize them by heating them in a moderate oven (160°C/325°F/Gas 3) for 20 minutes, boiling them for 10 to 15 minutes, or putting them through an otherwise-empty dishwasher cycle (don't add detergent). Whichever method you use, make sure the jars are completely dry but still warm when you add the jam: putting hot jam into a cold jar may cause it to crack.

Makes: 2 kg (4½ lb)

INGREDIENTS
1 kg (2¼ lb) prepared fruit
(plum, strawberry, fig, or apricot)
1 kg (2¼ lb) white granulated sugar
1½ tablespoons lemon juice
1 cinnamon stick (fig jam only)

- Prepare the fruit first, by washing it and removing any stones. Cut the flesh into small pieces and weigh.

- Add the fruit to a large pan and place over a medium heat. Cover the pot until the fruit begins to simmer, then remove the lid, add the sugar and lemon juice (and cinnamon if making fig jam), and continue to simmer until the jam is cooked. To test: Put a drop of jam on a plate and allow it to cool slightly, then pick some up between your thumb and forefinger to feel if it is sticky. If there is no resistance between your thumb and forefinger, continue cooking, checking regularly. When the jam is sticky, remove from the heat (and remove any cinnamon). Remove the jars from the heat source carefully using tongs: Do not touch the opening or the inside with your hands. Carefully fill the hot, sterile jars (see opposite) with the hot jam.

- Cover the jars with waxed disks (wax-side down) and cellophane tops; secure with clean elastic bands and the jar lid. As the jam cools it will create a vacuum, making an airtight seal.

- Leave the jars to cool before storing. When opening, make sure there is no growth on the surface of the jam and keep refrigerated after opening.

Keeka bi-goz el-hend | Moist Coconut Cake

This delicious butter and coconut cake served as our birthday cake more often than not because it is just so good. Even now, when I am well into adulthood, the smell of this cake brings back fond memories. I don't think my siblings or I ever realized that our birthday cakes were made from this one cake because mum would color it using food coloring, then ice and decorate it differently each time. We could also request a chocolate cake, which my mum would then produce by adding cocoa to the same mix, so there was never a shortage of possibilities to make each birthday cake unique. My mum would produce a perfect, aerated, moist cake and I have had real difficulties in trying to replicate it without knowing the original quantities. This recipe is as close as I can get—it may not be identical, but it is pretty good nevertheless. Use an electric mixer for a lighter, fluffier cake.

Makes: 1 large or 2 small cakes

INGREDIENTS
300 g (10½ oz) self-raising flour, plus extra for dusting
6 eggs
1 teaspoon vanilla extract
225g (½ lb) sugar
1 cup (250 ml) whole milk
250 g (9 oz) unsalted butter, plus butter for greasing
90 g (3 oz) desiccated coconut

- Preheat the oven to 160°C (325°F/Gas mark 3). Lightly grease a 30 by 25 cm (12 by 10 inch) cake tin with butter and lightly coat with flour (invert and shake to remove excess flour).
- Place the eggs and vanilla in a large bowl and beat for about 3 minutes, until the eggs are light and fluffy. Add the sugar and continue to beat together until well combined—about another 3 minutes.
- Start adding the flour and milk—add half a cup of flour at a time, and alternate with a little milk, until all the flour and milk is added. Scrape down edges as you go.
- Slowly add the melted butter, then the coconut, and beat until well combined. Transfer the mixture to the prepared tin and bake for 50–60 minutes, until golden on top and cooked though (a skewer inserted into the center should be clean when removed). Leave to cool slightly before turning onto a wire rack to cool fully.

VARIATION

To make a chocolate-coconut cake, sift 2–3 tablespoons of cocoa powder with the flour before adding it to the egg mixture.

Basbousa bi-l-loz | Semolina Cake with Almonds

Basbousa is a cake made with semolina—the gritty, coarse particles of wheat left after the finer flour has been extracted. Traditionally, it is served with tea and coffee, and it is one of many Egyptian sweets that relies on a final coating of cooled sugar syrup to soften and sweeten it. If you were to ask three different people how they make *basbousa*, there would be three different replies. My sister-in-law's mother makes it with yogurt and baking powder, while my mum made hers with milk and self-raising flour. This recipe uses lots of almonds, for a high nutritional value and a rich taste. Whether making *basbousa* with almonds, yogurt, coconut, or a combination of these, you are bound to receive many compliments from those lucky enough to sample it. This is a very easy sweet to prepare and is always enjoyable to eat.

The syrup can be flavored with vanilla or edible flowers, by using dried lavender (see *Variation*, below), rose water, or orange blossom water. These can be combined with a dash of vanilla or it can be omitted altogether. I have tried all these flavors, but nothing beats vanilla for me. *Basbousa* can be stored in an airtight container at room temperature for a day or two.

Makes: 24

INGREDIENTS

250 g (9 oz) semolina
225 g (8 oz) sugar
250 g (9 oz) unsalted butter,
    plus extra for greasing
1 cup (250 ml) milk
140 g (5 oz) self-raising flour
15 raw almonds, skins removed and halved

Syrup
400 g (14 oz) sugar
2 cups (500 ml) water
Juice of half a lemon
3–4 drops of vanilla extract or
    1–2 tablespoons rose/orange blossom water

- Begin by making the syrup. Combine the sugar, water, and lemon juice in a small pan, bring to the boil, then turn down the heat and simmer for 10 minutes or until the syrup is thick enough to coat a spoon. Leave to cool. Once cooled, add the vanilla or flavored water and stir.

- Preheat the oven to 180°C (350°F/Gas mark 4). Lightly grease a 30 by 25 cm (12 by 10 inch) cake tin with butter.

- Place the semolina and sugar in a large bowl and combine. Melt the butter, then add this to the bowl along with the milk and flour, mixing well after each addition.

- Transfer the cake mixture to the baking tin. Cut it into 24 squares and place the almond halves in the center of each square. Place in the oven and bake for 50–60 minutes or until golden brown.

- Remove the basbousa from the oven and carefully pour the cold syrup evenly over the hot cake. The temperature difference between the syrup and cake results in greater absorption, so don't be tempted to leave both to get to room temperature. Serve when the cake has cooled.

VARIATION

I once made this with lavender syrup using a bunch of lavender grown and given to me by my gorgeous friend Karen. I kept the fresh lavender until it dried, but you can buy the dried flowers from many supermarkets and delicatessens. To use, take about 2 tablespoons of the dried lavender (use buds that have not opened—look for those that are deep purple and tightly wrapped). Add them to the water, sugar, and lemon when making the syrup then strain them out after it cools.

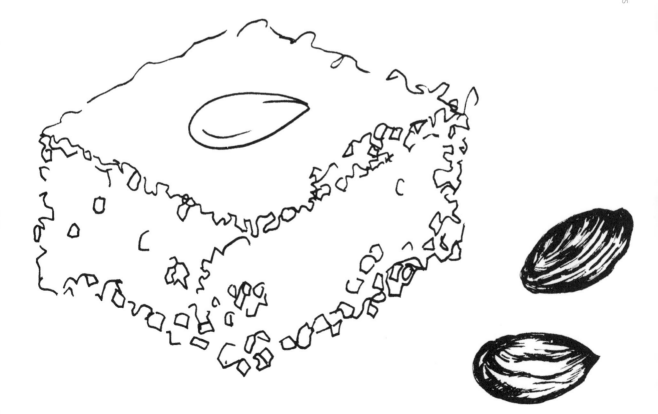

Basbousa bi-goz el-hend | Semolina Cake with Coconut

People who love coconut will find that this version of *basbousa* definitely hits the spot. The coconut flavor is mild but noticeable and the coconut helps to add texture. You could also play with the texture of the *basbousa* by using fine, coarse, or half-and-half semolina. I prefer to use half-and-half as I prefer the texture particular to the fine semolina, which produces a denser result.

Makes: 24

INGREDIENTS
250 g (9 oz) unsalted butter,
    plus extra for greasing
375 g (13 oz) semolina
225 g (8 oz) sugar
170 g (6 oz) desiccated coconut
1½ cups (375 ml) milk

Syrup
450 g (1 lb) sugar
2 cups (500 ml) water
Juice of half a lemon
1 teaspoon coconut essence, optional

• Begin by making the syrup. Combine the sugar, water, and lemon juice in a pan. Bring to the boil, then reduce the heat and simmer for 10 minutes until the syrup reduces and thickens. Remove from the heat and add the coconut essence (if using), stir, and leave to cool.

• Preheat the oven to 180°C (350°F/Gas mark 4). Lightly grease a 30 by 25 cm (12 by 10 inch) cake tin with butter. Melt the remaining butter, pour it into a large bowl, add the semolina and mix well.

• Add the sugar, coconut, and milk. Mix well to combine. Transfer the mixture to the baking tray, press firmly to flatten, and cut into squares or diamonds to make 24 cakes.

• Place in the oven and bake for 50–60 minutes or until golden brown.

• Remove the *basbousa* from oven and leave to cool for about 5 minutes before pouring over the cool syrup. Serve with whipped cream, if desired.

Basbousa bi-l-zabadi | Semolina Cake with Yogurt

This is another tasty variation of *basbousa*. While still containing dairy, the yogurt is thicker and adds a little tartness, which balances out the sweetness a little. I have also made this using a store-bought, vanilla-flavored yogurt (I'm sure I've mentioned that I'm a big vanilla fan). It strengthens the vanilla flavor from the syrup and fills the house with the most beautiful aroma while in the oven.

Makes: 24

INGREDIENTS
125 g (4½ oz) coarse semolina
125 g (4½ oz) fine semolina
225 g (8 oz) sugar
1 teaspoon baking powder
250 g (9 oz) natural yogurt
125 g (4½ oz) unsalted butter,
    plus extra for greasing

Syrup
400 g (14 oz) sugar
2 cups (500 ml) water
Juice of half a lemon
3–4 drops vanilla extract

• Begin by making the syrup. Combine the sugar, water, and lemon juice in a pan. Bring to the boil, then reduce the heat and simmer for 10 minutes until the syrup reduces and thickens. Add the vanilla and leave to cool.

• Preheat the oven to 180°C (350°F/Gas mark 4). Combine the semolina, sugar, baking powder, and yogurt in a large bowl. Melt the butter and mix it in thoroughly.

• Lightly grease a 15 by 25 cm (6 by 10 inch) cake tin with butter, add the mixture, and press firmly into place. Cut the mixture into squares or diamonds to make 24 cakes.

• Place in the center of the oven for 50–60 minutes or until golden brown. When cooked, remove the cake from the oven, and pour the cooled syrup over the warm basbousa.

COOK'S TIP

The *basbousa* mixture can be prepared a day ahead, kept in the refrigerator, and then baked when you want it.

Dairy-free Basbousa

My daughter is on a dairy-free diet and has been since she was two months old. I was completely taken by surprise after her appointment with the paediatrician and wondered how I would ever manage without using all my dairy favorites in cooking. Eliminating butter, cheese, milk, and yogurt took considerable adjustment, but fortunately it also resulted in the discovery of very tasty (and slightly more healthy) meals and treats. This was one of them. I was apprehensive about serving dairy-free *basbousa* to my family, but need not have worried—I was thrilled when my stepmother Nehad told me it was the best *basbousa* she had ever tasted—what a compliment!

Makes: 24

INGREDIENTS
340 g (12 oz) fine semolina
225 g (8 oz) sugar
170 g (6 oz) desiccated coconut
125 g (4½ oz) vegetable oil spread
1½ cups (375 ml) soy milk
1 teaspoon vanilla extract

Syrup
450 g (1 lb) sugar
2 cups (500 ml) water
Juice of half a lemon
1 teaspoon vanilla extract

- Begin by making the syrup. Combine the sugar, water, and lemon juice in a pan. Bring to the boil, then reduce the heat and simmer for 10 minutes until the syrup reduces and thickens. Leave to cool.

- Preheat the oven to 180°C (350°F/Gas mark 4).

- In a bowl mix together the semolina, sugar and coconut. In a separate bowl or jug, heat the vegetable spread until soft.

- Add the soy milk and vanilla extract, and mix together well.

- Pour the wet ingredients into the dry ingredients and mix together well. If the mix is dry, add a little more soy milk. Pour into a 30 by 25 cm (12 by 10 inch) cake tin. Spread evenly, place in the oven, and bake for 50–60 minutes or until golden brown.

- Remove the *basbousa* from the oven and pour over the cool syrup. Cut into squares and serve.

Ba'lawa | Baklava

This well-known sweet is popular all over the Mediterranean and has become well known in Australia and the USA too. The crunchy nuts and pastry are a great combination with the sticky, sweet syrup. You can give the baklava a very distinctive flavor by adding rose water, orange blossom water, or honey to the syrup, but I like it with just a hint of vanilla.

The key to the success of this dish is to brush each sheet of pastry really well with melted ghee. This adds flavor but, more importantly, provides a crispness to the layers. Butter can be used in place of ghee, but be careful when cooking it because the milk solids in butter can easily burn, which will ruin your baklava. Caution is necessary in several ways when using filo pastry: The sheets are very thin and can tear easily, but the greatest danger is the sheets drying out and becoming brittle. This would make working with the sheets very difficult, as they would begin to fall to pieces. Place a slightly damp tea towel over the unused sheets as you work to prevent the sheets from drying out.

Traditionally baklava is made with chopped nuts, which give it a rich taste and add to the crispy, crunchy texture, but I enjoy the contrasting texture of sultanas or currants scattered throughout. You can add lots of these or just a few—or omit them entirely if you prefer.

Makes: 24 squares

INGREDIENTS
225 g (8 oz) pistachios, walnuts,
   or almonds, coarsely chopped
60 g (2 oz) sugar
1 teaspoon ground cinnamon
½ teaspoon ground cloves
1–2 tablespoons sultanas or currants (optional)
250 g (9 oz) ghee, plus extra for greasing
375 g (13 oz) filo pastry, at room temperature

Syrup
400 g (14 oz) sugar
2 cups (500 ml) water
Juice of half a lemon
3–4 drops vanilla extract

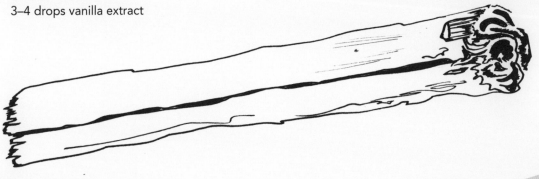

- Begin by making the syrup. Combine the sugar, water, and lemon juice in a pan. Bring to the boil, then reduce the heat and simmer for 10 minutes until the syrup reduces and thickens. Add the vanilla and leave to cool.

- Preheat the oven to 180°C (350°F/Gas mark 4). In a bowl, combine the chopped nuts, sugar, cinnamon, cloves, and any sultanas or currants.

- Lightly grease the base and sides of a 30 by 25 cm (12 by 10 inch) cake tin with ghee. Melt the remaining ghee.

- Take the filo sheets from their packaging and place them on a chopping board or plate, then cover the filo sheets with a damp tea towel. Remove a single sheet of filo pastry at a time. Taking the first sheet, fold it in half and place it in the tray. Brush the top with melted ghee and fold in the edges to fit, if necessary. Repeat this process for half of the filo sheets, making sure you brush each sheet with ghee, and folding the sides where necessary to fit the tray.

- Sprinkle the nut mixture over the pastry in the tray and then continue to layer the pastry with the remaining sheets, following the same process as before. When you have used all the sheets, pour any remaining ghee over the top.

- Cut the layered pastry into 24 diamond or square shapes, making sure to cut right through to the base.

- Place in the center of the oven and bake for 20–25 minutes or until the baklava is puffed and lightly golden on top.

- Remove from the oven and pour the cooled syrup over the hot baklava. Leave to cool before cutting along the diagonals again to remove from the tray.

COOK'S TIP

This can be prepared one day and baked the next. Cover and store the layered pastry in the refrigerator overnight and bake shortly before you want to eat it. Baklava will also keep for several days after baking in an airtight container at room temperature: Do not store it in the refrigerator after baking or the sheets will go soggy.

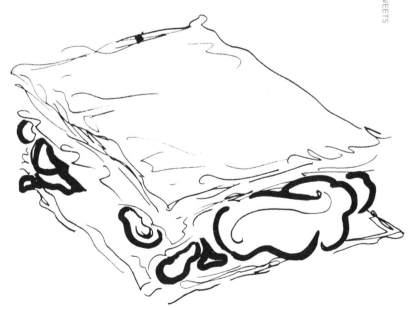

Konafa bi-l-ishta | Konafa with Double Cream

Konafa is a pastry soaked in wonderfully sweet syrup. The name refers both to the finished dish and to the spun pastry used—called *kadaif* by the Greeks and the Turks—and it is made using a dough from wheat flour in much the same way as filo pastry. The finish is entirely different though, because the pastry is prepared by pouring the dough through a funnel or perforated disc to form very thin strands which are channelled onto a hot metal plate that dries them instantly. The final product resembles malleable angel hair pasta. It can be molded into shapes, filled with chopped nuts and sugar, then baked into crunchy deliciousness. *Konafa*, or *kataifi*, pastry can be bought in Mediterranean grocers or delicatessens. I went so far as organizing for my local supermarket to start stocking it!

The double cream used in this particular *konafa* recipe makes for quite a rich and heavy dessert that's not very healthy but quite irresistible. I grew up thinking that *ishta* was the skin on top of milk that is formed after milk is heated and cooled—I now know that it is the thick layer of cream that sits on top of fresh milk. It works perfectly in this recipe, but double cream or clotted cream are good store-bought options if you don't have a handy cow to provide fresh milk and the amazing cream that sits on top. Unsalted butter can be used as a substitute for ghee, but ghee is preferable because it can be heated to a higher temperature than butter before it starts to burn.

This is not how we had *konafa* at home, as my mother would routinely make *konafa* with nuts (see page 142), but I do remember having it once like this and absolutely loving it, so I set about making a replica from memory. This means that the version here may or may not be traditional; either way, it tastes both decadent and delicious.

Makes: 20 portions

INGREDIENTS
1 tablespoon cornstarch
1½ tablespoons sugar
2 cups (500 ml) milk
250 g (9 oz) ghee or unsalted butter
375g (13 oz) konafa
½ cup (125 ml) double cream
100 g (3½ oz) ricotta cheese,
    at room temperature

Syrup
225 g (8 oz) sugar
1 cup (250 ml) water
Juice of half a lemon
3–4 drops vanilla extract

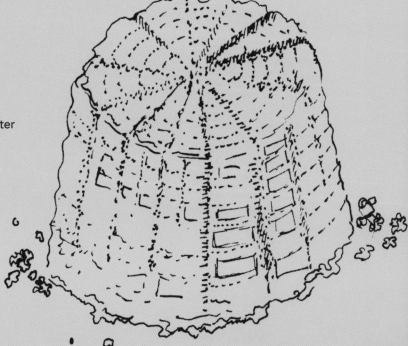

- Begin by making the syrup. Combine the sugar, water, and lemon juice in a pan. Bring to the boil, then reduce the heat and simmer for 10 minutes until the syrup reduces and thickens. Add the vanilla and leave to cool.

- Preheat the oven to 180°C (350°F/Gas mark 4). Mix the cornstarch and sugar in a cup with ¼ cup of the milk until smooth. Heat the remaining milk in a pan and when just coming to the boil, add the cornstarch mixture. Turn down the heat and stir continuously while the milk is simmering until it thickens. Leave to cool, then add the cream, and combine well.

- Melt the butter or ghee. Put the pastry strands in a bowl and pour melted butter over them, then mix thoroughly with your fingers to coat and completely separate the strands.

- Put half the buttered pastry into a 30 by 25 cm (12 by 10 inch) baking dish and flatten with the palm of your hand. Pour the cream mixture over the top and then crumble the ricotta on top of the cream. Cover with the remaining pastry.

- Place in the center of the oven. Bake for 45 minutes at 180°C (350°F/Gas mark 4) then increase the temperature to 230°C (450°F/Gas mark 8) for a further 10 minutes or until the *konafa* is golden in color.

- Remove the *konafa* from the oven and pour the cooled syrup over the top. Leave it to cool down to room temperature, then cover with a plate and turn over to remove. Cut and serve hot or cold.

COOK'S TIP

Konafa freezes very well and just needs to be brought back to room temperature before use. This can be done by leaving it for a couple of hours, covered, on a worktop, or by heating it gently in a microwave until soft.

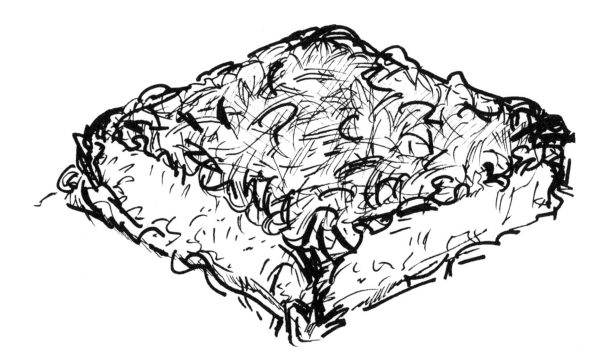

Konafa bi-l-mikassarat | Konafa with Mixed Nuts

My mum was an expert at making *konafa* (see page 140), which she twisted around a nut filling and placed into a round tin to create a wondrous spiral. The recipe here is the much easier and far less time-consuming cake style that I make, but feel free to experiment with various shapes or patterns. You can use just one kind of nut or a combination of two or three to suit your own taste. You can also add a couple of tablespoons of rose water or orange blossom water to the syrup if you like, in addition to, or instead of the vanilla essence. If it doesn't all get eaten at once, cover the *konafa* with plastic wrap and keep at room temperature; do not store in the refrigerator or the pastry will go soggy.

Makes: 1 cake

INGREDIENTS
225 g (8 oz) pistachios, walnuts,
   or almonds, coarsely chopped
3 tablespoons sugar
1 teaspoon ground cinnamon
½ teaspoon ground cloves
375g (13 oz) konafa
250 g (9 oz) unsalted butter or ghee

Syrup
225 g (8 oz) sugar
1 cup (250 ml) water
Juice of half a lemon
3–4 drops vanilla extract

- Begin by making the syrup. Combine the sugar, water, and lemon juice in a pan. Bring to the boil, then reduce the heat and simmer for 10 minutes until the syrup reduces and becomes thick enough to coat a spoon. Leave for 5 minutes to cool, then add a few drops of vanilla essence and stir.

- Preheat the oven to 180°C (350°F/Gas mark 4). Combine the nuts, sugar, and spices in a bowl.

- Pull apart the filo or *konafa* strands in a bowl and pour melted butter over them. Mix thoroughly with your fingers to coat and separate the strands.

- Lightly grease a large, deep, round dish (diameter around 25 cm/10 inches) and put half the pastry into it. Flatten the pastry with the palm of your hand. Spread the nut mixture evenly over it and cover with the remaining pastry. Flatten the top again.

- Put into the center of the oven and bake for 60–65 minutes or until golden in color. Remove the *konafa* from the oven and pour the cooled syrup over the top. Leave it to cool to room temperature, then cover with a plate and turn over to remove. Cut and serve.

COOK'S TIP

The *konafa* may be made into individual portions by separating the strands, placing some nut mixture at the end of each one, and rolling each stuffed strand into tight little logs. Place these on a tray cut-side down before baking for 20–25 minutes, and drizzle 1 or 2 tablespoons of syrup over each.

Roz bi-l-laban | Rice Pudding

This is the old-fashioned type of rice pudding where you cook the rice with the milk, rather than add pre-cooked rice to milk. The result is a hearty, creamy dish. My twist on this classic dessert is to make it using coconut milk. It tastes so good, I don't make the original any more. We used to eat it at home for breakfast or as a snack. Extra pudding can be placed in bowls, covered, and kept in the refrigerator until wanted, then warmed in the microwave with a little extra milk. To serve, sprinkle with chopped nuts, sultanas, or cinnamon. It is also delicious drizzled with pure maple syrup—go on, pour it from a height just for the drama!

Serves: 4

INGREDIENTS
2 cups (500 ml) milk
2 cups (500 ml) coconut milk
170 g (6 oz) short-grain white rice
60 g (2 oz) white sugar, or as desired
40 g (1½ oz) butter
½ teaspoon almond essence or vanilla extract
Cinnamon, sultanas, or chopped almonds, to decorate

- Pour the milk and coconut milk into a heavy-based pan and place over medium heat. Bring just to the boil, then add the rice and reduce the heat. Cook uncovered, at a simmer, for 30–35 minutes, or until the rice is tender. Stir the rice occasionally to prevent a skin from forming on the surface. Add extra milk or water if all the liquid is absorbed before the rice is cooked through.

- When cooked and creamy, add the sugar and stir well until dissolved.

- Take the pudding off the heat and stir in the butter and almond or vanilla flavoring. Transfer to serving bowls and drizzle with maple syrup or sprinkle with cinnamon, sultanas, or chopped almonds—or all of these—if desired.

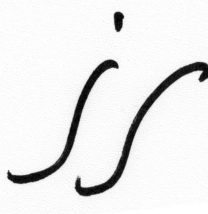

Sha'riya bi-l-laban | Noodles with Milk

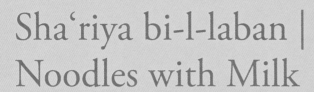

Sha'riya bi-l-laban is similar to rice pudding but made with noodles. It is commonly eaten in Upper Egypt and in rural villages, where they usually use wheat dough to make long thin strands of noodles, which are dried before use, and buffalo milk. I have never seen the noodles made and have not tried making them myself—I use dried wheat noodles I find in the Asian or international food aisle of the supermarket. If you toast the noodles to a brown color before putting them in the milk they impart an almost nutty flavor to this dish, and I think it's well worth taking the time to do so. Or just toast half of them; this will give you a whole spectrum of colors, from white to brown, and add great visual interest as well as flavor.

Serves: 4

INGREDIENTS
250 g (9 oz) dried wheat noodles
5 cups (1¼ liters) milk
115 g (4 oz) sugar, or as desired
60 g (2 oz) butter
1 teaspoon vanilla extract

• Preheat the oven to 200°C (400°F/Gas mark 6). Wrap the noodles in a clean tea towel and use a meat mallet or rolling pin to break them up.

• Place all the noodle pieces on an oven tray—even the little bits. Bake in the oven for 10–15 minutes, turning occasionally, until noodles are mostly browned. It is better to have more of them brown than creamy colored, but don't overcook and burn them, and don't worry if some are not as browned as others.

• While the noodles are toasting, place the milk and sugar in a medium-sized pan and heat on medium heat until hot but not boiling.

• Remove the noodles from the oven and add to the hot milk. Reduce the heat to a low simmer and cook for 15–20 minutes or until the noodles are soft, stirring occasionally and breaking up any lumps as they cook and soften. Keep an eye on the milk to make sure it doesn't boil over.

• When cooked, remove from the heat and stir in the butter and vanilla extract. Serve immediately with a little extra milk, if desired.

COOK'S TIP
This dish will keep in the refrigerator, covered, for a day or two; just add a little milk before reheating in a microwave or pan.

Mihallabiya bi-l-amariddeen | Apricot Summer Pudding

Amariddeen is a kind of fruit leather—it is a sticky, apricot thick paste that can be bought in strips or folded like a letter inside bright orange cellophane. In the West, it can be found in Mediterranean delicatessens and Middle Eastern grocery shops, but it is common throughout the Middle East. It was a childhood favorite, and as kids we sometimes just ripped bits off and ate it. *Amariddeen* can be dissolved in water and served as a cool drink in summer (page 170) or it can be combined with cornstarch to make a delicious summer pudding, as here.

Serves: 4

INGREDIENTS
350 g (½ lb) *amariddeen*
3 tablespoons cornstarch
1 tablespoon sugar, or as desired
Nuts, cream, or vanilla yogurt, to decorate

- Place the *amariddeen* in a large bowl and cover with 2 cups (500 ml) water. Leave to dissolve for several hours or overnight, stirring occasionally, until the apricot leather becomes a thick liquid.
- In a cup, mix the cornstarch with ¼ cup (60 ml) water to form a smooth paste.
- Place the apricot liquid in a pan and bring to the boil over a medium heat.
- Add the cornstarch paste, reduce the heat to a simmer, then add the sugar. Stir continuously until thickened.
- Divide the apricot pudding among 4 ramekins or bowls, and leave to cool before refrigerating. Decorate with nuts, cream, or vanilla yogurt before serving.

Mihallabiya | Almond Custard

This sweet is made from corn and rice flour but is similar to custard in consistency, hence the name. It is served cold, so it is refreshing on warm summer nights. You can vary the quantity or ratio of the flours in this recipe if a different consistency is desired. As with most things, the flavor can be altered as well depending on what you add. I prefer to use vanilla to flavor sweet dishes because I just love it, but if you like the flavor of orange blossom or rose water, try substituting 2–3 tablespoons of one or other for the vanilla.

Serves: 4

INGREDIENTS
2 tablespoons rice flour
2 tablespoons cornstarch
4 cups (1 liter) milk
115 g (4 oz) sugar, or as desired
3–4 drops vanilla essence
100 g (3½ oz) ground almonds
Chopped pistachios or blanched almonds, to decorate

• Combine the flour and cornstarch and mix with ¼ cup (60 ml) milk to make a smooth, thick paste.

• Add the sugar to the remaining milk, place this in a pan, and bring just to the boil over medium heat.

• Reduce the heat and add the flour paste gradually, stirring constantly so it does not boil, for 10–15 minutes until there is a slight resistance and the mixture coats the back of the spoon.

• Add the vanilla essence and cook for a further 2 minutes. Remove from the heat and stir in the ground almonds.

• Cool a little before dividing into individual ramekins or glasses. Refrigerate for 3 or 4 hours and serve decorated with chopped almonds or pistachios, if desired.

Zalabya | Syrup-drenched Donuts

Zalabya are perfect for those with a sweet tooth. These lovely golden balls of sweetness are made by deep-frying dough and then, as with so many Egyptian sweets, soaking them in thick sugar syrup. The donuts are very similar to the Greek *Loukmadis*—which are soaked in a honey syrup. *Zalabya* are great for a large gathering where there will be plenty of people to enjoy them. They also have a wow factor that makes them fun for dinner parties.

Makes: approximately 50

INGREDIENTS
2 teaspoons dried yeast
1 teaspoon sugar
140 g (5 oz) plain flour, sifted
Corn oil, to deep fry

Syrup
400 g (14 oz) sugar
2 cups (500 ml) water
Juice of ½ lemon
4–5 drops vanilla extract

• Begin by making the syrup. Combine the sugar, water, and lemon juice in a pan and place over a medium heat to dissolve the sugar. Bring the syrup just to the boil and simmer for 10 minutes. Turn off the heat and leave to cool. Place the yeast, sugar, and 2 tablespoons of the warm water in a cup. Stir then leave in a warm place for 10 minutes until bubbles form. (If there are no bubbles it means the yeast is dead and you will need to start again with fresh yeast.)

• Sift the flour into a large bowl, make a well in the center, and add the yeast. Add 1 cup (250 ml) warm water and mix together to form a smooth consistency. Cover the batter with a tea towel and leave to rise in a warm place for 2 hours or so until the dough doubles in size. The time will depend on the temperature—the batter will need a warm, not hot, environment to rise.

• Heat the oil in a deep-fryer over high heat. When the oil is just starting to smoke, drop a teaspoonful of the batter into the hot oil. It should immediately expand in size. Add several spoonfuls, so you are cooking a few *zalabya* at a time. When they have turned golden brown on one side, turn them over.

• When each batch is cooked, remove the donuts and place them directly into the syrup, turning them over to make sure they are fully coated. Leave for a few minutes then remove from the syrup and drain in a colander or sieve over a bowl. Repeat for each batch. Serve immediately.

COOK'S TIP

It is best to be very organized before beginning to fry the *zalabya*. Position the dough close to the oil so that you are not reaching over to get it. Place the syrup next to the oil on the other side so that you can easily remove the donuts with a long, slotted spoon or tongs and dunk them in the syrup. Next to the syrup, place a colander sitting over a bowl, with another slotted spoon or tongs, for draining the syrup from the donuts. When one batch of *zalabya* are sitting in syrup, dip the next few into the oil—only remove those sitting in the syrup just before the next batch is ready to come out of the oil.

Krem Karamel | Crème Caramel

Crème caramel is traditionally a French dessert, but ever since the occupation of Egypt by the French between 1798 and 1801, Egyptians have cooked and adapted a few typically French dishes. (They also learned the French language—my parents learned both French and Arabic at school.) This is one of those dishes; a simple yet satisfying baked custard that can be made in individual ramekins or in a large bowl to share. Turn the custard onto a plate after baking to release the gold-colored caramel and let it cascade over the custard.

Serves: 4

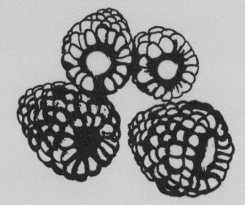

INGREDIENTS
Vegetable oil, for greasing
225 g (8 oz) caster sugar
4 eggs
1 teaspoon vanilla extract
3 cups (750 ml) milk
Pouring cream (optional), to serve
Fresh or frozen berries (optional), to serve

• Preheat the oven to 160°C (325°C/Gas mark 3). Put on a full kettle of water to boil—you will need this for making the water bath.

• Lightly brush a large ovenproof dish (about 6 cups/1½ liter capacity) with oil or 6 individual ramekins.

• Begin making the caramel. Place ¼ cup (60 ml) water and 155 g (5½ oz) sugar in a small pan over medium heat. Keeping watch to avoid burning the caramel, cook without stirring for 8 minutes, or until the caramel has reached a warm, golden color. Allow the bubbles to subside, then pour the mixture evenly among the ramekins or in the larger ovenproof dish. Swirl several times to coat the base and about halfway up the sides of the dish. Set aside.

• While the caramel is cooking, whisk together the eggs, vanilla, and remaining sugar in a large heatproof bowl. Pour the milk into a medium-sized pan and place it over low heat. Bring it just to the boil then remove from the heat and slowly add the hot milk, whisking constantly until the mixture is well combined.

• Pour the milk mixture carefully over the caramel in each ramekin.

• Place the ramekins or large dish into a roasting pan. Pour enough boiling water into the roasting pan to reach halfway up the side of the dish. Bake for 40 minutes or until the custard is just set.

• Remove the custards from the water bath and set aside for 2 hours to cool.

• To serve, run a flat-bladed knife around the inside edge of each ramekin and carefully invert the crème caramels onto a serving plate. Serve with cream and berries, if desired.

COOK'S TIP
Crème caramel can be prepared ahead of time. After cooking, allow it to cool, then cover with plastic wrap and place in the refrigerator overnight. Gently heat until warm so that the caramel flows over the custard.

Atayef | Crunchy Syrup Pillows

Atayef are ultra-delicious. Beautifully crunchy, these nut-filled pillows are drenched in sugar syrup. They can be time-consuming to prepare, but they are definitely worth the effort, especially if you want to impress guests at your next dinner party. In trying to perfect this recipe I found out why this sweet was not a regular feature in our household, and remembered how my mother and I once worked in the kitchen for many hours trying to get the batter to the right consistency. My mum made this dish so rarely that she had completely forgotten how to make it, and for the first time I can remember, she began a method of trial and error until finally we (but more importantly she) had produced the sweet in exactly the way she remembered.

Atayef are best served immediately when they are sweet and crunchy, so only fry what you need or they will become soggy. They may be prepared up to the frying stage and kept covered in the refrigerator for a few hours until required, or even frozen. Remember to completely thaw these out completely before frying or the oil will splutter when they are fried.

Although this is not the traditional approach, I have found that by using a non-stick frying pan, without butter or oil of any kind, it is possible to produce a pancake that is not greasy and will seal very easily after being stuffed with nuts. This is essential, because if the pancakes are not sealed properly they will open when being fried and the stuffing will comes out and burn. You can use any nuts here: Raw walnuts, almonds, pistachios, or mixed nuts all work well.

SWEETS

Makes: 30–35

INGREDIENTS
170 g (6 oz) crushed walnuts
1 tablespoon sugar
2 tablespoons sultanas (optional)
1 sachet (7 g) dried yeast
1 teaspoon sugar
225 g (8 oz) plain flour
Corn oil, for deep-frying

Syrup
400 g (14 oz) sugar
2 cups (500 ml) water
Juice of ½ lemon
1 teaspoon vanilla extract

- To make the stuffing, combine the crushed walnuts, sugar, and sultanas together in a small bowl. Set aside.

- To make the syrup, combine the sugar, water, and lemon juice in a pan, bring to the boil over a medium heat, then lower the heat and cook for 8–10 minutes. The syrup should be a thin consistency. When cooked, remove from the heat and leave to cool. Once cooled, add the vanilla and stir. Set aside.

- While the syrup is cooking, make the dough. Place the yeast, sugar, and ¼ cup (60 ml) warm water in a cup, stir, then leave in a warm place for 10 minutes until bubbles form. (If there are no bubbles the yeast is dead and you will need to start again with fresh yeast.)

- Sift the flour into a large bowl, make a well in the center, and add the yeast mixture. Add 1½ cups (375 ml) warm water and use your fingers to mix together a dough that is smooth and consistent. Cover with a tea towel and leave to rise in a warm place for 1–2 hours until the dough doubles in size.

- Heat a non-stick frying pan on medium heat without oil or butter. Mix the dough with a dessert spoon and then use the spoon to collect about half a spoonful of dough and place it into the frying pan. Spread it thinly and evenly to a 10 cm (4 inch) diameter—like a small, slightly thicker kind of crepe. Cook on one side only, and remove from the heat when the dough has changed from white to yellow. Place on a clean dish and repeat until all mixture has been used.

- Place a teaspoon of the stuffing into the center of each pancake on the uncooked side. Fold over each one, pressing the edges firmly together, to form a half moon.

- Heat the oil in a deep-fryer over high heat. Test for the correct temperature by placing a dough scrap in the oil—it should bubble entirely over the dough immediately. Carefully place 2 or 3 *atayef* into the oil at a time, and fry until golden brown in color, turning as required.

- Remove each one from the oil as it is cooked and place it directly into the cooled syrup, turning to coat. Remove from the syrup and leave to drain in a colander or sieve. When they are all cooked, serve immediately.

VARIATION
You can leave the pancakes flat and deep-fry them without stuffing. They taste great, especially when accompanied with double cream and fresh fruit such as strawberries or blueberries.

Khoshaf | Dried Fruit Compote

This dessert comes from the Arabian Gulf but it is something we used to have at home occasionally in summer. It is a relatively healthy dessert when compared to many sweets from the Mediterranean because it is made by rehydrating dried fruit. The fruit can be pretty much whatever you want to use; apricots, plums/prunes, figs, dates, sultanas, peaches, and pears all work well (remember that there may be stones remaining in the prunes so take care when eating them).

The fruit can be topped with almonds and walnuts if you want to add texture—in this version of the recipe I've included pomegranate seeds for a modern twist that adds color and texture. I like to add cream, too, because it cuts through the sweetness of the fruit and gives the compote a lovely creaminess. This dessert is a wonderful way to end a meal on a hot summer night, as it is sweet and served cold.

Serves: 4

INGREDIENTS
450 g (1 lb) of dried fruit, such as apricots, figs, or peaches
4 tablespoons double cream or crème fraîche
1 tablespoon pomegranate seeds

• Place the dried fruit in 4 cups (1 liter) water and leave to soak in the refrigerator overnight. If you need to prepare the dish on the same day as eating it, place the fruit in a pan with the water and place over medium heat until just boiling. Simmer for 30 minutes or until the dried fruit is plump and juicy. Remove from the heat and leave to cool before serving.
• Place the rehydrated fruit into a dish and garnish with cream and pomegranate seeds.

COOK'S TIP
I find this dish quite sweet without adding sugar, but if you like your desserts very sweet you could make a simple sugar syrup by dissolving some sugar in water, then pouring it over the fruit.

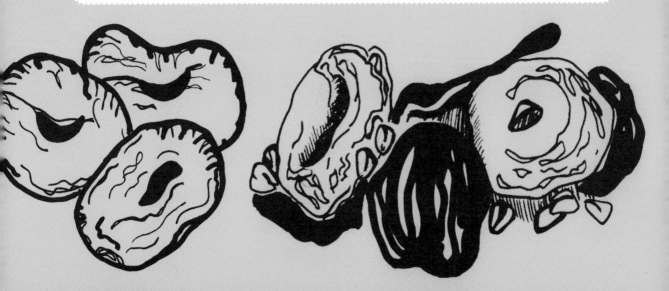

Kowar el-shokolata | Mum's Chocolate Truffles

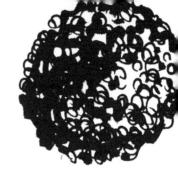

When I was growing up, there was only one thing better than my mum's coconut cake (page 130)—her version of chocolate truffles, which she made with the leftover cake. Of course this involves not eating the whole cake in the first place, but once you've got over that hurdle this recipe is very easy, as the cake will dry out the older it gets, so converting it to tasty chocolate balls is simple. It also meant that in our house, no cake was ever wasted.

Personalizing these is easy. You can add dried fruit or nuts to the truffle mix as you like—chopped nuts, glacé cherries, sultanas, currants, or even dried cranberries or blueberries work really well. Finish by rolling the truffles in colored sprinkles, dessicated coconut, chocolate shavings, or crushed peanuts.

Makes: approximately 24

INGREDIENTS
½ Moist coconut cake (page 130)
2–3 tablespoons cocoa powder
3–4 drops rum or vanilla essence (optional)
200 g (7 oz) unsalted butter, melted
56 g (2 oz) desiccated coconut

- Crumble the cake into a bowl and add the cocoa powder. Gently mix together.
- Add the rum or vanilla essence to the melted butter and pour the mixture over the cake crumbs.
- Gently stir together, then divide the mixture into balls the size of walnuts, and roll each one in dessicated coconut (or a finish of your choice) to decorate.
- Refrigerate for at least 15 minutes before serving.

COOK'S TIP

For an even easier version, mix 300 g (10½ oz) crumbled cake with rum or vanilla essence and ½ cup (125 ml) sweetened condensed milk. Wet your palms in water to roll and finish as above.

Gullash bi-l-kastard | Pastry Custard Squares

This is similar to a custard tart and it is a very easy dessert to prepare if you use store-bought filo pastry. It also makes a refreshing alternative to baklava (page 138) when you don't feel like eating syrup-drenched sweets.

Every time I think of this dish I remember the first time my husband-to-be came to our family home. It was during the university holidays, and the thought that he was coming over made me giddy with excitement and quite nervous. I asked my mum what I should make for him, because I felt that some part of the dinner should be made by me. We decided on this as the perfect ending. I can't remember now what we had for the rest of the meal, but I clearly remember bringing this out and serving it as the last dish. What I hadn't anticipated was that my future husband was so careful to please my parents that he had eaten the entire, huge mound of food put before him at dinner and so had absolutely no room left for anything else. In the end I told him that I had made it especially for him, so he ate a piece—truly just to keep me happy.

Makes: 20–24 squares

INGREDIENTS
125 g (4¼ oz) unsalted butter
1 packet filo pastry
5 eggs
1½ cups (375 ml) milk
2 tablespoons sugar
3–4 drops vanilla extract
Icing sugar, to dust

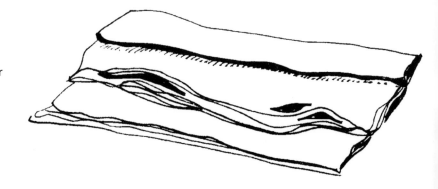

• Preheat the oven to 180°C (350°F/Gas mark 4). Melt the butter, then use some of it to lightly grease a 30 by 25 cm (12 by 10 inch) oven tray.

• Take a single sheet of filo pastry and, starting lengthways at one end, gather up the pastry in folds so that it ends up as a long, narrow shape. Place the gathered pastry in the baking tray and repeat the process until all the sheets of pastry have been gathered up and placed side by side in the tray. Fill in the sides and gaps of the tray, then cut the large pastry shape into squares.

• Pour the remaining butter over the pastry, and bake in the oven for 15 minutes or until the pastry is crisp and lightly golden.

• While the pastry is cooking, beat together the eggs, milk, sugar, and vanilla.

• When the pastry is golden in color, remove it from the oven, pour the egg mixture over it, and bake for a further 10–12 minutes. Remove from the oven, sprinkle with icing sugar, re-cut the squares, and serve.

Teen | Walnut-stuffed Figs

When I think of these I think of my dad. He loved to open a packet of dried figs and start cutting them in half, stuffing each one with a walnut. I love the crunch of the walnut with the popping of the fig seeds and the way the sugar in the fig is balanced by the oil in the walnut. These would be fantastic served as part of a cheese platter, alongside fresh summer fruits, or simply on their own as a simple yet satisfying snack in the evening.

California walnuts are slightly more expensive than Chinese walnuts but they are less bitter, so it may be worth spending a little more to use the Californian ones for this simple treat.

Serves: 4

INGREDIENTS
8 dried figs
4 walnuts, shelled and halved

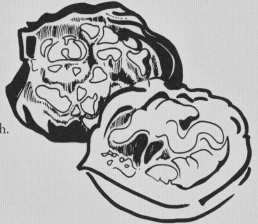

- Halve the figs horizontally but not all the way through.
- Place half a walnut in the center of each fig and serve.

Fitir | Sweet Flaky Pastry

This pastry is made from scratch and takes several hours to prepare, so I would recommend setting aside half a day and devoting yourself to the task. The labor involved may explain why ancient Egyptians served this as an offering to the gods, though today it is a popular pastry throughout the Middle East. We didn't often have it at home, mainly because it is laden with butter (if you are watching your cholesterol, enjoy this in moderation). In fact, you won't want to eat very much of it in one sitting—it is so filling, a little goes a long way. It is ideal for gatherings and can be prepared either as a sweet or as a savory pastry, because the topping is entirely up to you. Feta cheese works well, and can be teamed up with tomatoes, figs, or whatever else takes your fancy. My favorite version is sweet and simple—lots of cream and fresh berries.

My strongest memory of *fitir* is eating this with my aunt and uncle when my husband and I visited them. As we had flown over 9,320 miles (15,000 km) and were staying with them for a week, we were being thoroughly spoilt. My aunt made the *fitir* one morning and as it was such an effort we waited patiently but hungrily to eat it, missing breakfast and lunch, until finally at around 2 pm we sat down to some wonderfully fresh butter pastry with a huge array of toppings. I ate at least a week's worth of calories at that meal and felt so full that I didn't eat again until the following morning.

Serves: 6–8

INGREDIENTS
450 g (1 lb) plain flour
Pinch of salt
450 g (1 lb) butter
½ cup (125 ml) cream
Raspberries, to serve (optional)
Double cream, to serve (optional)
Icing sugar, to serve

- Combine the flour and salt in a bowl and add enough warm water to form a ball of dough. Knead it until it becomes elastic, then roll it into a ball and set aside, covered, for 30 minutes.

- Shape the dough into 5 balls then cover and rest again for 30 minutes.

- Heat the oven to 180°C (350°F/Gas mark 4). Take the first ball of dough and roll it out using a rolling pin until it forms a flat, thin circle. Lift the piece of dough and place a tablespoon of butter and one of cream onto your worktop or bench then place the dough on top.

- Add 1 tablespoon each of butter and cream to the center of the dough circle and use your fingers to stretch out the dough still further—you're aiming for almost a paper-thin sheet.

- Fold the left-hand edge into the center, then fold the right-hand edge into the center (on top of the last fold). Then lift the bottom edge up to the center, and lastly the top edge down over the folded dough. You should now have a small square of folded dough (this is called the 'envelope').

- Take the second ball of dough, and place it on top of 1 tablespoon each of butter and cream, as for the first piece of dough. Roll it out very thinly as for the first piece of dough. Now place the first envelope into the center of the second sheet. Add another tablespoon each of butter and cream on top of the envelope, then fold the second sheet from the left, right, bottom, and top again to make a larger envelope.

- At this stage the two envelopes have become one. Roll the third ball into a sheet with butter and cream then add the large envelope into the center. Repeat the process until all the balls of dough have been used.

- Leave the layered dough to rest for 30 minutes, then place it on a pizza tray. Add another tablespoon each of butter and cream on top, then spread the dough out again using your fingers— aim to spread it to the edge of the tray.

- Place in the oven and bake for 30 minutes or until golden in color. Remove, cut into wedges, and serve with berries and cream sprinkled with icing sugar.

Kuskusi | Sweet Couscous

We ate this for breakfast occasionally but also as a snack any time of the day. It is incredibly quick to make in a microwave—simply put the couscous in a microwave-safe bowl with the water and cook on high heat for a few minutes until the water is absorbed and the couscous is cooked.

Serves: 1

INGREDIENTS
45 g (1½ oz) couscous
½ cup (125 ml) water
1 tablespoon butter
Icing sugar, to serve

- Put the couscous in a bowl and pour boiling water over it. Cover and leave it for 10 minutes or so, until the water has been absorbed and the couscous is cooked.
- Add one tablespoon of butter and mix through.
- Sprinkle with icing sugar to taste, and mix in or leave on top as desired.

Pettifore | Petits Fours

These are great cookies and very popular. They can be tricky to make and are quite time-consuming, but they are well worth the effort. They're also really fun to make with family or friends. I remember my parents sitting together and chatting while assembling these. Dad would match the cookies for size, spread them with jam, and join them together, then pass them to my mum who dipped them in melted chocolate and chopped nuts or chocolate sprinkles and set them aside to dry.

I love these after they have sat for a day and the cookie has had time to absorb some of the jam, becoming ever so slightly sticky. *Pettifore* keep well in an airtight container out of the refrigerator and are so more-ish that I can never stop at just one. You can showcase them to their full glory by placing them under a covered glass display stand.

Makes: 30–50

INGREDIENTS
225 g (8 oz) unsalted butter, plus extra for greasing
200 g (7 oz) caster sugar
1 egg
½ teaspoon vanilla essence
350–500 g (12–18 oz) self-raising flour
Strawberry or raspberry jam, for filling
250 g (9 oz) cooking chocolate, melted
Crushed peanuts, for coating (optional)
Chocolate sprinkles, for coating (optional)

- Preheat the oven to 160°C (325°F/Gas mark 3).

- In an electric mixer, beat the butter until light and fluffy. Add the sugar and beat until combined, then add the egg and beat it into the mixture.

- Add the vanilla and then start adding the flour, a little at a time, scraping down the sides as you go, until the mixture is just coming together to form a ball. It should still be quite soft.

- Lightly grease a baking tray with butter. Roll the mixture into 30–40 walnut-sized balls and place them well apart on the tray. Dust your hands with flour and then flatten the balls with your fingers, to cookie thickness. You can also make lines, dots, or indentations with a fork to create different patterns.

- Bake for 12–15 minutes or until the cookie base is lightly golden. Remove from the oven, leave for 2 minutes, then carefully take them off the tray using a metal spatula.

- Once cooled, divide the balls into pairs of roughly even sizes. For each pair, spread jam on one cookie and then put the other cookie on top.

- For an especially delicious finish, dip a third or half of the paired cookies into melted chocolate and coat with crushed nuts or sprinkles. Serve or store in an airtight container.

VARIATION

To make chocolate cookies, take half the mixture and place it in a clean bowl. Gently fold in 1 or 2 tablespoons of cocoa. To give the cookies a marbled look, add only 1 tablespoon of cocoa to the entire mixture and gently fold it through just a few times, leaving it only partially mixed in.

Kahk |
Icing Sugar Shortbread Cookies

These cookies are laden with butter and sugar, so they are quite heavy and sweet. I used to make these and take them to work sometimes, where they were all quickly gobbled up, but at home they were popular at celebrations such as Christmas and Easter. In Egypt these are an essential component of the Muslim *Eid el-Fitr*, the feast after Ramadan (the month in which Muslims fast from sunrise to sunset). The shortbread is so popular then that when *kahk* is noticeably being baked and purchased by a vast majority of Arab Muslims, it is an indication of the arrival of Eid.

Kahk is said to have originated in ancient Egypt during the Eighteenth Dynasty (1540–1307 BCE). Back then it was made using honey and flour, pressed into discs, decorated with the imprint of the sun's rays, and then baked. Numerous different pictures of this ancient Egyptian sweet decorate the inner walls of Kheime Ra's tomb in Thebes, near the modern city of Luxor.

Kahk fillings can vary; favorites includes nuts—such as pistachios, walnuts, and almonds—or Turkish delight *(malban)*. *Kahk* with pitted, puréed dates *('agwa)* is more common in other parts of the Arab (where it is known as *ma'mul*).

Makes: 20

INGREDIENTS
250 g (9 oz) unsalted butter, softened, plus extra for greasing
45 g (1½ oz) icing sugar, plus extra to coat
1 egg yolk
¼ teaspoon vanilla extract
1 teaspoon baking powder
75 g (2½ oz) self-raising flour
140 g (5 oz) plain flour, plus extra
70 g (2½ oz) crushed walnuts or almonds

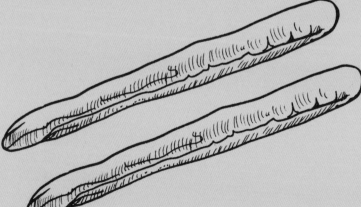

- Preheat the oven to 180°C (350°F/Gas mark 4). Lightly grease two oven trays and cover with baking parchment.

- Beat the butter and icing sugar in an electric mixer until light and fluffy. Add the egg yolk and vanilla and beat well to combine.

- Sift the baking powder and flours together. Gradually add this to the butter, along with the nuts, and combine. The mixture is ready when it comes together as a ball of dough. Remove from mixer and place on a floured board.

- Form the dough into little balls about the size of walnuts and flatten slightly with a fork. Alternatively, mold into thin sausages about 10 cm (4 inches) long and 1 cm (½ inch) wide, then bring the ends together to form a horseshoe shape. Place the dough shapes on to the baking trays, allowing room for spreading, and bake for approximately 10 minutes or until the cookies are slightly browned on the base.

- Remove from the oven and leave for a few minutes before sifting a little icing sugar over the top. Remove to a cooling rack to cool completely. When cooled, sift extra icing sugar on to them so they are well coated. Store in an airtight container out of the refrigerator, if there are any left!

Ghurayiba | Butter Cookies

These are lovely cookies that are made in Egypt at Christmas and during the Muslim feast of Eid el-Fitr. At Christmas, my mother would spend a day making a range of cookies including *ghurayiba*, which would be served with tea and coffee to our visitors and given away in containers. I was always astounded by the large number of cookies that she made at Christmas but it certainly ensured that there was never a shortage and by the end of the festive season there were just enough for us to enjoy a few ourselves.

Makes: 20–25

INGREDIENTS
250 g (9 oz) butter, softened, plus extra for greasing
80 g (3 oz) icing sugar
½ teaspoon vanilla
1 tablespoon vegetable oil
½ teaspoon baking powder
250–275 g (9–10 oz) plain flour
20–25 whole cloves, or whole almonds, peeled and roasted

• Preheat the oven to 180°C (350°F/Gas mark 4). In a mixing bowl, beat together the butter, icing sugar, and vanilla. Add the oil and baking powder, then gradually add the plain flour until the dough forms a ball that comes away from the bowl.

• Shape the mixture into small balls the size of hazelnuts and place on a greased tray, well spaced out. Place a single whole clove or almond in the center at the top of each ball. Bake for 15 minutes then remove. These should not be browned on the base—remove them early if they begin to brown. Leave the cookies to cool before serving them or storing them in an airtight container.

Biscote shamar | Cookies with Fennel

I love these cookies, and not just because they are a distant relative of the modern-day version. Unlike so many cookies nowadays, they are not too sweet, but they do have a lovely aroma and great crunch. Even if the idea of fennel seed in a cookie doesn't appeal, I encourage you to give these a try anyway—you are sure to be pleasantly surprised.

I enjoy dipping these in a cup of hot chocolate or coffee but they are just as good on their own. This recipe produces a large quantity but any leftover cookies will keep really well in an airtight container and will not spoil quickly.

Makes: 40–50

INGREDIENTS

5 eggs
¼ teaspoon vanilla
225 g (8 oz) caster sugar
1 tablespoon fennel seeds
¾ cup (180 ml) vegetable oil, plus extra for greasing
450 g (1 lb) plain flour
450 g (1 lb) self-raising flour
½ teaspoon baking powder
½ cup (125 ml) milk

- Preheat the oven to 160°C (325°F/Gas mark 3). Place the eggs and vanilla in a large bowl and beat together.

- Add the sugar, fennel, and oil, and beat until well combined.

- Sift the flours and baking powder together. Add the milk and the flour to the egg mixture, stirring only with a spoon until combined. Use only as much flour as required to make the dough just come together.

- Lightly grease a baking tray with oil and use a spoon to place 2 or 3 lengths of dough about 10 cm (4 inches) long on the tray. Transfer to the oven and bake for 15–20 minutes then remove.

- Cut the half-baked cookies into 1 cm (½ inch) slices and place them on a baking tray lying on their sides. Reduce the oven temperature to 150°C (300°F/Gas mark 2) and bake for a further 15 minutes.

- Turn off the oven and leave the cookies in the oven to dry. Once cooled, keep in an airtight container and serve with tea or coffee.

COOK'S TIP
This recipe makes a large quantity of cookies but the dough freezes well, so you could freeze half of it for cooking another time. Thaw well before shaping and baking.

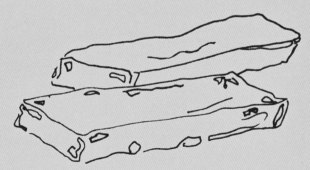

Biscote nashader | Ammonia Cookies

These cookies are deliciously light and crunchy and made using ammonia—but not the household cleaning kind! Baker's ammonia is made of ammonium carbonate, so this is actually an ancestor of modern baking powder. If you can't locate baker's ammonia, you can make your own substitute: 1 teaspoon of baker's ammonia requires the equivalent of 1 teaspoon of baking powder plus 1 teaspoon of baking soda.

These cookies are a specialty of my stepmother. Her cookies turn out so beautifully that I eagerly look forward to Christmas, when she makes them in abundance and generously passes some on to me. This recipe makes heaps of cookies, and although numbers will vary depending on the size you make them. You can also make them into all sorts of shapes using a piping bag and nozzle. The cookies keep best if stored in an airtight container.

Makes: 20–25

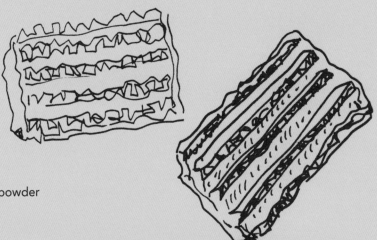

INGREDIENTS
6 eggs
½ teaspoon vanilla
225 g (8 oz) caster sugar
1 cup (250 ml) vegetable oil
½ cup (125 ml) milk
1 tablespoon baker's ammonia powder
450 g (1 lb) plain flour
450 g (1 lb) self-raising flour

- Preheat the oven to 180°C (350°F/Gas mark 4). In a large mixer bowl, add the eggs, vanilla, and sugar and beat for 5 minutes until light and fluffy.

- Add the oil and beat together. Combine the milk and ammonia powder in a cup, then add to the mixture.

- Sift the flours together and gradually add to the egg mixture. If using an electric mixer, beat on slow speed until the mixture is thick and comes away from the bowl.

- Lightly grease and line three baking trays with baking paper. Take 1 heaped teaspoon of dough at a time and shape it into a ball, then place on the baking tray. Repeat until you have used all the mixture.

- Using a fork dipped in flour, lightly flatten each cookie until it is around 1 cm (½ inch) thick. Place in the oven and bake for 15–20 minutes or until lightly golden.

- Remove from the oven and allow to cool on the trays for 10 minutes. Then transfer to a wire rack to cool completely.

Biscote goz el-hend | Coconut Drops

My dad remembers having these when he was a child. They are so easy to make that children can make them too and generally love to do so. In my house they are a quick and easy party favorite or yummy afternoon treat.

Makes: 24

INGREDIENTS
250 g (9 oz) desiccated coconut
400 g (14 oz) condensed milk
Red or green glace cherries, quartered

• Preheat the oven to 150°C (300°F/Gas mark 2). In a large bowl, combine the coconut and condensed milk, and mix well.

• Line a baking tray covered with baking parchment. Using wet hands, roll teaspoons of the mixture into balls the size of walnuts and place on the tray, leaving plenty of space between each one. Press down on the top of each ball using fingertips or a fork to flatten slightly.

• Position a cherry piece on the top of each cookie. Place the baking tray in the oven and bake for 15 minutes, then increase the heat to 180°C (350°F/Gas mark 4) for a further 5–10 minutes, or until golden brown.

• Leave to cool for 5 minutes on the tray, then use a metal spatula to transfer the cookies to a wire rack to cool completely.

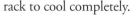

ʿAseer amariddeen | Apricot Juice

The main ingredient of this drink is an apricot paste known as *amariddeen*, or 'fruit leather.' It can be found in Middle Eastern grocers and some delicatessens. We used to drink this in summer as children, because it is sweet and refreshing, but it is popular all over the Middle East during Eid el-Fitr, the holidays just after Ramadan. It can be made to suit any taste by adding more or less sugar for sweetness, and varying the amount of water to produce different consistencies.

Serves: 4

INGREDIENTS
350 g (12 oz) *amariddeen*
2 cups (500 ml) water
1 tablespoon sugar

- Cut the sheets of *amariddeen* into pieces. Place in a large bowl and cover with water. Leave overnight.
- Transfer the apricot liquid and any undissolved pieces of amariddeen into a large pan. Add the sugar and heat on medium heat for 5 minutes, stirring constantly.
- Reduce the heat and simmer for a further 3 minutes stirring constantly. Pour the liquid into a jug and leave to cool before placing in the refrigerator. Serve cold.

Karkadeh | Hibiscus Tea

Karkadeh is a tea known for its remarkable ruby red color and subtle floral flavor. It has been produced in Egypt for centuries and it is made from the dried sepals that form around the seed-pods of the Roselle, or *Hibiscus sabdariffa* flower.

This tea has been enjoyed since the time of the ancient Egyptians, who drank it hot in winter and cool as a refreshing drink in summer. Roselle flourishes in the climate and environmental conditions found in Egypt, and the plant gives this tea a rich, dark, almost purple-black color and a wonderfully floral aroma and flavor. It is overflowing with health benefits. In fact, *karkadeh* is drunk in Egypt mainly for its medicinal benefits—recent scientific studies have confirmed that it is high in Vitamin C and antioxidants, and helps to reduce blood pressure in people with diabetes or high blood pressure. When buying the dried roselle (also sold as hibiscus flowers), look for the dark variety—the light-red kind has less flavor and contains more acid.

Serves: 4

INGREDIENTS
1 small handful dried hibiscus flowers
2–4 heaped teaspoon sugar, as desired

- Add 4 cups (1 liter) cold water to the dried flowers in a pan and bring to the boil.
- Reduce the heat and simmer for three minutes.
- Strain the bright red liquid into a teapot or jug. Add a teaspoon of sugar (or to taste) for each glass, stir, and serve hot.

COOK'S TIP

For a lovely cool drink in summer, place the dried flowers in a jug, pour over some boiling water, add sugar to taste, and stir until the sugar dissolves. Leave until the water becomes dark red. Strain the tea and cool in the refrigerator until serving.

Ahwa | Arabic Coffee

Ahwa is served in espresso coffee cups along with a selection of cookies and it is popular all over the Arab world. It was the kind of coffee we had with guests, and so perhaps it is no coincidence that it was in the company of visitors that I tried my first cup of real coffee. I remember a wonderful family friend coming to visit when I was a teenager and on this particular occasion he requested 'proper' coffee. I don't remember what gave me away, but for some reason it became apparent that I didn't know to how to make it. Well . . . this was a situation that needed to be rectified immediately, and so I learned how to make 'proper' coffee, or *ahwa*. The skill lies in producing a thick layer of foam or *crema* on the top. One way to increase the foam is to pour slowly and try to lift the pot higher and higher as the pouring continues.

I find that one of the most common misunderstandings about this kind of coffee in my cooking classes has been about the coffee grind itself. Arabic or Turkish coffee depends more on the exceptionally fine grinding of the beans than the growing place of the beans. Its unique taste and texture also owes much to the fact that the ground coffee is boiled. Espresso coffee also uses finely ground coffee beans, but it is made by forcing hot water through the grounds, so the major difference lies in the brewing method.

The method given here is for basic coffee, but feel free to experiment: the addition of some cloves or cardamom pods during cooking really changes the flavor. And while this coffee is traditionally drunk without milk, I love a dash of Irish cream liqueur in my coffee once in a while. A standard espresso coffee cup holds 90 ml, so it is the perfect measure of the amount of water required per person.

Serves: 1

INGREDIENTS
1 espresso cup (90 ml) water
1 heaped teaspoon Arabic/Turkish coffee
1 heaped teaspoon sugar

• In a long-handled coffee pot, measure the water required for the number of people drinking, allowing 1 espresso cup of water per person. Add the coffee and sugar in equal proportions, and stir until the coffee sinks and the sugar is dissolved.

• Place the coffee pot over low heat for 3 minutes or so until the coffee begins to rise (do not stir it once it is on the heat). Just before it boils, remove it from the heat. When the foaming diminishes, return the pot to the heat, then as it starts to boil, remove and pour into cups. Serve immediately.

COOK'S TIP

All the coffee from the pot is poured into cups, so this includes the coffee grounds, but these drop to the bottom of the cups to form a thick layer of sludgy grounds—do not drink these (something I neglected to inform my husband the first time he had Arabic coffee).

CONVERSION TABLES

All cooks have their favorite methods of working, and this includes measuring devices. Some people love to work in cups, while others prefer to measure on scales; the conversion tables below are a quick and easy way to check one form of measurement against another. I have also included a guide to oven temperatures for reference.

Measuring fluids		
Metric	**Cup**	**Imperial**
30 ml		1 fl oz
60 ml	¼ cup	2 fl oz
80 ml	⅓ cup	2¾ fl oz
100 ml		3½ fl oz
125 ml	½ cup	4 fl oz
150 ml		5 fl oz
180 ml	¾ cup	6 fl oz
200 ml		7 fl oz
250 ml	1 cup	8 fl oz
310 ml	1¼ cups	10 fl oz
375 ml	1½ cups	13 fl oz
430 ml	1¾ cups	15 fl oz
475 ml		16 fl oz
500 ml	2 cups	17 fl oz
625 ml	2½ cups	21 fl oz
750 ml	3 cups	26 fl oz
1 liter	4 cups	35 fl oz
1.5 liters	6 cups	52 fl oz
2 liters	8 cups	70 fl oz

Measuring weight	
10 g	⅓ oz
15 g	½ oz
30 g	1 oz
60 g	2 oz
90 g	3 oz
115 g	4 oz
140 g	5 oz
170 g	6 oz
200 g	7 oz
225 g	8 oz
255 g	9 oz
285 g	10 oz
310 g	11 oz
340 g	12 oz
370 g	13 oz
400 g	14 oz
425 g	15 oz
450 g	1 lb
750 g	1½ lb
1 kg	2¼ lb
1.5 kg	3⅓ lb
2 kg	4½ lb

Oven temperatures				
Celsius (electric)	Celcius (electric fan)	Fahrenheit	Gas	
140°	120°	275°	1	Cool
150°	130°	300°	2	
160°	140°	325°	3	Moderate
180°	160°	350°	4	
190°	170°	375°	5	Moderately hot
200°	180°	400°	6	
220°	200°	425°	7	Hot
230°	210°	450°	8	
240°	220°	475°	9	Very hot

INDEX

ACKNOWLEDGMENTS

I would like to thank many people for their input and support during the writing of this book, particularly my family, including my siblings and Marian and Joussian. My mum, Mary, was my primary inspiration for the book and we spent many hours talking about the recipes and working in the kitchen together. I give my highest praise and thanks to my dad, who has been incredibly helpful and supportive, not only during my work on this book but throughout my whole life. I am thankful I have you as my dad. I love you and thank you for helping shape who I am today. Following my mother's passing, my stepmother, Nehad, has been invaluable. Nehad, for all the hours you have spent talking me through recipes, correcting my errors, allowing me to join you on Christmas biscuit baking days, and laughing through it all, I am eternally thankful. I found a joy in cooking these dishes as a result.

Thank you, too, to my friends Marie, Nat, Sue, Diem, Karen, and Peter and Jacinta, for their encouragement and support over the many years, as well as my in-laws, Lyn, David, and Aunty Val, who have followed my journey with interest and assisted with so much.

To my links in the publishing world, Julie and the senior editor, Nadia, for getting all my years of hard work across the finishing line, I am very grateful to you both. I want to thank Trevor Naylor and AUC Press for taking the project on. It has made my cookbook dream a reality and one of my life's wishes come true, and for that I am grateful.

To the many others who have enquired about the progress of the book over the past decade, I am glad to finally say I have finished. I hope that you will find any time you spend reading, shopping for, or cooking the recipes in this book an enjoyable experience.

And finally, to my husband, Jamie, and my children, Alexander and Samuel and Tahlia. I love you *awy-awy*. I am grateful for your love and support in all areas of my life, but I cannot thank you enough for all your help, including but not limited to the shopping, cooking, and cleaning up and eating anything and everything I plated up. It has not always been easy, but I hope the journey has been as rewarding for you as it has been for me. To my darling babies, I hope you will cherish and enjoy the food of your heritage, passed on from your grandmothers and mum. With all my love now and for your future.

ILLUSTRATION CREDITS

All drawings are by Niki Medlik.

Thanks to Maher, Karim, and Mohammed and the Haider shop of Norwich for the Arabic handwriting and all their help and advice.

The publisher would like to thank the following for permission to use their photographs in this book:

Trevor Naylor: *page 2 (top)*; Doriana MacMullen: *2 (bottom: left and right); 15 (bottom), 29 (center), 30, 35, 37, 38, 49, 51, 57 (bottom), 59, 62 (right: top and center), 69, 75, 89, 95, 97, 99, 102–103, 105, 108, 113, 115, 117, 119, 121, 124, 127, 131, 161, 169, 173, 176, 182–83*; Sarah Praill: *6 (top)*; Niki Medlik: *6 (bottom)*; Renee Robinson: *9*; Nancy Abdel Messieh: *10, 15 (top), 17, 23 (top), 24, 25, 26, 28 (left), 42, 47, 57 (top), 60, 62 (left; right: bottom), 63, 71, 73, 93, 126, 132, 135, 143, 151, 171*; Dyna Eldaief: *19, 23 (bottom), 28 (right: center and bottom), 29 (top and bottom), 54, 136, 144, 148, 152, 155, 159*; James Buntine: *28 (right: top), 129, 163*; Nadia Naqib: *81.*